# FROM CHARITY TO CREATIVITY

## PHILANTHROPIC FOUNDATIONS
## IN THE 21st CENTURY

Perspectives from Britain and Beyond

By

Helmut K. Anheier and Diana Leat

First published in the UK in November 2002 by Comedia

Copyright © Helmut Anheier and Diana Leat

A catalogue record for this book is available from the British Library

ISBN 1 837667 16 7


Comedia,

The Round, Bournes Green,

Near Stroud, GL6 7NL, UK

e-mail charleslandry@comedia.org.uk

http://www.comedia.org.uk

Book layout & design Gabrielle Boyle


Commissioned by

The Joseph Rowntree Reform Trust

The Garden House

Water End

York YO30 6WQ

01904-625744


Printed and bound by Da Costa Print/The Book Factory

Pims House, Mildmay Avenue,

London N1 4RS


This and other Comedia publications available through

Eco-Distribution, Crosswell, Crymych,

Pembrokeshire, SA41 3TE

0123 989 1431

jill.chandler@virgin.net

# Contents

# Foreword

Philanthropic foundations are regarded as important hallmarks of civil society in Britain. They constitute a valuable resource, which is independent of government, and they are generally well regarded.

But, compared with the United States, relatively little is known about British trusts and foundations, the way they work or about any measured outcomes resulting from their largesse. The milieu in which they operate is cosy enough and allows them to be as anonymous as they wish. It has not altered noticeably for the past century. Governing bodies generally are comprised of self-perpetuating oligarchies serviced by tenured staff, though more recently consultants of one variety or another have been commissioned to advise on specific projects. Some foundations, sometimes in some of their work, have been genuinely innovative. Such new developments derive usually from their staff and occasionally from the prompting of trustees, but it is more often the case that the world of philanthropy goes about its business much as it has always done, beyond the gaze of the public.

A significant influence contributing to the prevailing state of affairs has been the stance that government has adopted towards philanthropic institutions. Their official regulator, the Charity Commission, is essentially no more than an invigilator, ensuring that they do not breach the parameters set by charity law and bringing any transgressions to book. The Commission investigates the occasional fraud –usually confined to the smaller local charity sector -and seeks strict compliance of the rules forbidding foundations from engaging in any kind of activity that could be construed as "political" in any sense. These have been rigorously enforced, though of late there has been some slight relaxation of the definition, so that a measure of campaigning (though strictly non-party political) is now permissible. The Charity Commission, then, can only perform a re-active, guardian-type role and is positively prevented by statute from being pro-active in any significant way. A major consequence is that there is no external stimulus to exhort or prod foundations into being more adventurous and pioneering in their endeavours, so, for example, as to encourage them to address the requirements of those clients and constituencies that have emerged more recently.

Some would argue, no doubt, that the current status quo is as it should be, but the validity of such a view needs to be demonstrated and not simply asserted. As the authors of this report show, there is any number of grounds to argue against such complacency and three, perhaps, are particularly compelling.

First, comparatively speaking, the history of philanthropy in the United States is altogether different. Unlike the British experience, it is characterised by a good deal of critical introspection by the foundation world itself and examination by government, both of which have led to considerable reform and change. US foundations are regarded as legitimate objects of scrutiny by academics, the media and legislators. It is a reasonable question to ask why British foundations have remained so immune from such public analysis of their activities and also to query whether this has been in the best interests of the foundations themselves.

Then, there are two, more specific, examples, which suggest that British foundations have not kept pace with changing reality. It is quite staggering to find in this report just how England-oriented UK foundations are in their focus –Northern Ireland, Scotland and Wales hardly get a look in. The over-whelming bulk of activity and expenditure is grotesquely and disproportionately biased in favour of England relative to the other parts of the United Kingdom. Similarly, it appears that the transformation of the country into a multi-cultural society has largely passed them by, given that only a relatively small amount of foundation expenditure has been allocated to the needs and aspirations of ethnic groups. Again, funding has not been at all commensurate. On both counts, British foundations seem to be locked in a time warp, increasingly lagging behind modern developments. Bearing in mind that forty per cent of their income derives directly, by way of exemption, from the tax-payer, it is legitimate to ask questions about both their modes of operation and how their missions might be made more relevant and creative.

This report raises many more issues for consideration but it only begins to scratch the surface. It is by way of a pilot study that nevertheless vividly illustrates the need for a much more detailed and extensive investigation. We need to know at least as much about British philanthropy as is known about US foundations and, more importantly, to open up a public dialogue about how it can best develop in the future. Foundations are a valuable community resource, which possess the potential to contribute much more value to civic society than they do. However, there are straws in the wind that may influence the future that need to be recognised now.

First, there is the advent of 'new' philanthropic money deriving from the vast fortunes of self-made multi-billionaire entrepreneurs. If history is anything to go by, these will inject new ideas and set out new directions while their buccaneering founders are at the helm. Much of that is long overdue and is to be welcomed but a caveat has to be entered. As large corporate business is increasingly influencing the shape of public policy, so the new charitable largesse may also seek to be another conduit of covert influence. One must hope this will not happen but we must be alert to the possibility.

Secondly, there has already arisen a related, almost reciprocal, problem and one that emanates from the state. Over the past decade, the practice has been developing whereby governments seek to finance specific public projects or programmes by inviting non-governmental funds -sometimes from business but also from charities – to contribute to the overall costs in some form of partnership; such augmentation has covered sports, the arts and educational and scientific projects.

Another factor in this trend has been the creation of the National Lottery. When it was launched government solemnly undertook that Lottery monies would not be used to finance projects that were previously regarded as the sole province of government and the public purse. That promise was quickly forsaken. Lottery funds, though not formally government controlled in the way they are disbursed, are nevertheless clearly heavily government influenced in the case of certain, usually large-scale projects as, for example, with not only the ill-fated Millennium Dome, but also for too many other ill-thought through millennial projects. If it gathers momentum, this trend towards partnership funding may well present a major problem. Philanthropy will be in danger of being co-opted, if not corrupted, by the state. The boundaries that hitherto have demarcated the civil sphere of society from the political sphere will be eroded, philanthropic independence will become compromised and agendas will be politicised.

This may be unduly alarmist and it is to be hoped so, but vigilance is needed given the portents. Like many long-established businesses that have not adapted with the times, many foundations are vulnerable to take-over, in effect by government co-option. If they have not been sufficiently innovative, initiatives will come, and indeed are coming, from elsewhere. The best antidote to prevent this from happening may well be along the lines suggested by Helmut Anheier and Diana Leat in this report. The authors make a compelling case to move away from the operating concept of the 'charitable foundation' of the nineteenth century, and its successor, the 'philanthropic foundations' of the twentieth century, towards the 'creative foundation' of the twenty-first century. Such a renaissance in philanthropy would have the potential of releasing a new energy, both intellectual and practical, placing foundations "at the crossroads of society rather than at its center", becoming "risk-taking" and "thinking the unthinkable". It is an exciting prospect.

And, finally, a codicil: why was the Joseph Rowntree Reform Trust Ltd (JRRT) persuaded of the need to take a look at British philanthropy and commission Dr Anheier and Ms Leat to undertake this investigation? The JRRT, a non-charitable endowed foundation, is a company limited by guarantee and as such pays taxes on its investment income, unlike charities which are tax exempt. It is therefore free to sponsor campaigns and political activities, including aspects of almost all the political parties in the UK. Its primary concern is to follow the directions of its founder, Joseph Rowntree, to help nurture democracy mainly in the UK, but which has been extended to include the European Union and occasionally beyond. He believed that political democracy can only thrive with a lively society alongside. Philanthropic foundations, as I remarked at the outset, are important components of that civil society which must not be allowed to ossify. The JRRT is part *of* the family of British trusts and foundations, but is not *in* it, precisely because it does not have charitable status. It is from this unique perspective – that of a candid relative, so to speak – that the JRRT decided to promote this study of its charitable counterparts with the aim of beginning a debate on the future of philanthropy in Britain which needs now to be taken much further by the foundations themselves.

TREVOR SMITH
(Professor Lord Smith of Clifton)

# Acknowledgments

This report owes its impetus to conversations with Tony Flower, Charles Landry and Lord Smith of Clifton about the current state of philanthropic institutions in the United Kingdom. A dinner meeting, hosted by Lord Smith at the Commonwealth Club in London in the Spring of 2001, brought several foundation experts together for a brain-storming session on 'what's good' and 'what's not so good' about organised philanthropy in this country. As an outcome of the meeting's lively discussion, the Joseph Rowntree Reform Trust Ltd commissioned a report from LSE's Centre for Civil Society on the future of organized philanthropy in the United Kingdom. The report was to offer both 'diagnosis and cure' and take a critical yet forward-looking approach in examining the state of foundations and charitable trusts.

We thank the Joseph Rowntree Reform Trust Ltd for giving us this opportunity to approach with fresh eyes a field we both have worked on for some time, and to engage, in the parlance and spirit of this report, in 'outside the box thinking' about foundations. We are grateful to Lord Smith of Clifton, Tony Flower and Charles Landry for their trust in our work and their support and input throughout the project.

A draft of the initial report was shared among colleagues and foundations experts, and heatedly discussed among a small group at the Reform Club. We thank Perri 6, Steven Burkeman, David Carrington, Andrew Crook, Nicholas Deakin, Jed Emerson, Elan Garonzik, Margaret Hyde, Barry Knight, Bernie Morgan, Christine Muskett, Nigel Siederer, James A. Smith, Volker Then, and Danielle Walker for reading an earlier version of this report and for providing useful comments, suggestions, and feedback. Clearly, not all reviewers agreed with our assessment, though most did, and while we took great care to accommodate their comments, final responsibility for this book and its content is ours alone.

Finally, we would like to thank Barbara Baum, Jane Schiemann, Sue Roebuck, and Lisa Carlson of LSE's Centre for Civil Society for their great assistance in the organisation and mechanics of this project.

# Executive Summary

## Précis

This report seeks to open up debate about the proper roles of philanthropic foundations in Britain and other advanced democratic societies. This is not a conventional research report. It is a combination of evidence, hypothesis and exhortation. Where possible we have drawn on available research but the existing information on foundations in Britain is simply insufficient to provide a solid, systematic picture of what this set of institutions does, how and for what purpose. As we argue below, more research is urgently needed, not least to support or refute our claims. By using a variety of empirical sources, some sounder than others, we want to challenge the conventional myths on which much of foundation legitimacy is based.

We raise critical questions about the current practice of organised philanthropy in Britain, and the aggregate achievements foundations have been able to make in this country and elsewhere. But we are relentlessly positive about the important roles of foundations in modern society. Our aim in this report was not only to encourage research, but also to provide a vision for a new and more robust justification for the continued role and heightened importance of foundations in a modern democracy. Some may agree with our argument; others may not. That is all to the good – we hope that other foundations will take up the gauntlet and support both further debate and research on the future of organised philanthropy.

We focus on endowed foundations, rather than charities in general, not because they have any special legal status but because endowed foundations are freer than charities without an independent, secure income to fulfil the roles we suggest are urgently needed in modern society. Our main argument is that the endowed, philanthropic foundation is a good and potentially vitally important institution in modern societies. Foundations fit in well with the way advanced democratic societies are developing, in particular with the nexus between private and public benefit in an era of 'small' government and greater social diversity. We also argue that foundations' current visions, roles, and, above all, organisational forms make it difficult for them to fulfil their promise. Against this backdrop, we develop a new vision and legitimate role for foundations based on their innovativeness and creativity.

In calling for greater 'creativity' we are not suggesting that foundations should simply continue their old-style passion for the new and so-called innovative, creating new offspring and then abandoning them after a year or two. When we suggest that foundations should be creative we mean that they should provide a space for alternative thinking, voices and practices. In a society in which government, business and the mainstream voluntary sector increasingly resemble each other and are driven by the short-term, often spurious, performance measures, foundations have a unique role to play in questioning the conventional wisdoms, making new connections, thinking and working 'outside the box'. Only foundations – not driven by customer, public fundraising and constituency demands – have the freedom to fulfil this role. They can become the intellectually active, independent and informed institutions that push innovation and social justice in modern societies. But it is a role that requires courage and long-term commitment. Without long-term commitment and discipline creativity can easily lapse into fad, fashion and crankiness.

We recognise that some foundations will feel unable to adopt a creative role – either because their deed is too narrowly drawn, or because they prefer to carry on as before filling gaps in existing provision. We accept the value of foundations' traditional charitable roles but argue that these roles do not play to foundations' unique strengths: their freedom to be creative in ways not open to other types of organisation.

We also argue that in the new policy context filling gaps in existing provision for health, social services, education or culture may turn out to be the thin end of a wedge foundations are ill-equipped to deal with. Becoming substitutes for state action, and being asked to shoulder responsibilities previously lodged with the public sector could easily threaten rather than encourage the full potential foundations have for modern societies.

Foundations need to find new and coherent roles that reflect changes in the environments in which they work. Foundations face new challenges, including questions regarding their accountability and legitimacy. They are in danger of having inappropriate roles and relationships thrust upon them by governments eager to privatise, and by businesses in search of quick fixes to demonstrate corporate responsibility. In an effort to demonstrate their usefulness, foundations are also in danger of becoming hostage to the politics of impact and performance measurement that will lead to technocratic control of their operations and spending rather than to the creative institution we have in mind.

Of course, accountability and transparency are vital aspects of any modern organisation, foundations included, but the emphasis on performance measures too easily prevented us from asking some of the more fundamental questions. What are the proper roles for foundations in the first place, and against what set of wider objectives do we judge their performance? We argue that unless foundations seize the significant opportunities open to them, and begin to articulate new and more positive roles that play to their strengths, e.g., their capacity for innovation and creativity, rather than their weaknesses, e.g., the risk of failure and the inability to demonstrate precise impact.

Analysts like Prewitt (1999) suggest that foundations' *raison d'être* is their contribution to pluralism. But this argument provides little defence for the significant privileges foundations enjoy, in particular their favourable tax treatment and their right to operate with a minimum of public oversight and accountability. Such privileges would be more justified if they made possible the *innovative pursuit* of pluralism. By having their assets and incomes exempt from taxation, and by moving them into a quasi-aristocratic position of patronage seemingly unaffected by modern institutional governance, foundations could become a vital source of social innovation and enhance the problem-solving capacity of modern societies. For example, foundations seek out fields—old, new or emerging—and identify issues and needs that can be supported by innovative ways and means.

The signature characteristic of foundations, namely, their specific capacity to innovate, is based on their freedom from the constraints of both the market and the state. Accordingly, their lack of democratic accountability is a virtue and the source of their freedom to innovate, or to support innovation, for the common good.

Certainly, not all foundations have to become, let alone remain, philanthropic innovators. Yet if the claim that they contribute to pluralism *and* innovation is to be borne out, they must be more than simple distributors of funds for specified causes and recipients. Foundations must be more than private and tax-sheltered mechanisms for distributing funds for worthy causes. Either their purpose or the approach taken must involve some value-added function that justifies the privileges afforded to foundations. That function is innovation, and specifically the innovative support of initiatives that serve the common good and contribute to pluralism.

Successful innovations typically show a distinctive set of characteristics: uncertainty, knowledge-intensity, controversy, and reaching across established boundaries. We link approaches to innovation to notions of creativity, and use Charles Landry's work on what makes cities successful and dynamic to develop a framework for the Creative Foundation of the future. We envisage a new type of foundation that is self-confident, not afraid to take risks, has strong intellectual leadership and operates on the basis of sound knowledge management, is entrepreneurial in its outlook as well as responsible and respectful, and, above all, embraces the diversity of modern society in seeking solutions.

The creative foundation of the 21st century represents the next evolutionary step in the continuing development of philanthropy from the charitable foundation of the 19th century through the philanthropic foundation to the 20th century. Creative foundations are interstitial institutions, located at the crossroads of society rather than in its centre; they are factories of ideas that bring about and facilitate innovation in the broadest sense. The creative foundation is a private problem-solving institution for public problems.

## Threats and Opportunities

Yet the very form of foundations makes it difficult for them to change and renew themselves in this direction. It is easier for foundations to remain conventional funding bodies set in their ways than to become flexible, change-oriented, and innovative. They tend to respond to pressures for renewal by becoming niche funders, addressing particular problems for specific clientele adopting predictable, stable patterns of disbursement, or following the fashion of the moment. However, the foundation world is operating in a changed and changing environment, which contains both threats and opportunities.

The threats foundations face include the increasing:

- loss of any coherent, dynamic, and defensible philosophy and roles;
- questioning of the effectiveness and efficiency of foundations— getting caught in the dominant performance-measurement culture;
- questioning of the value and legitimacy of foundations' privileged legal and fiscal position;

- demands for accountability and transparency;

- risk of having unrealistic roles imposed upon them by others, in particular through state devolution and privatisation; and

- risk of failure to achieve growth and self-renewal and to attract new philanthropists.


Opportunities include the chance to:

- develop new, more robust roles and rationales for foundations in an assertive way;

- redefine foundations' relationships with government in a positive and clear way;

- rethink foundations' governance and relationships in ways which would make them more vibrant and effective;

- resolve some of the fundamental dilemmas of policy and practice which have dogged foundations for decades;

- make a genuinely distinctive contribution to the public good which plays to foundation strengths rather than their weaknesses; and

- reinvigorate philanthropic foundation formation for the 21st century.


The critical challenge for philanthropic foundations is not merely one of money, or even fundamentally one of legitimacy. It is lack of creativity and the lack of both knowledge and awareness of interdependence. The ability of foundations to meet this challenge could provide the key to reinventing philanthropic foundations, their legitimacy, and their sustained growth. Creativity is the central issue for foundations today.

## Towards the Creative Foundation

Endowed foundations need to stop playing to their weaknesses and start playing to their strengths. But this requires honesty and 'out of the box' thinking. First, foundations have to acknowledge that they have neither the resources nor the democratic mandate to fill gaps, or to provide everything the state does not provide. What is more, they should no longer use resource limitations as an excuse to turn down grant-seekers, but should make it very clear that they are not in the business of doing what governments, market firms, or other non-profit organisations might do better. Foundations should stop pretending they could be more and do more only if they had more resources. Endowed foundations need to learn the three fundamental R's: *realism* about their resources relative to costs of provision; *rationalism* about the ways in which social change occurs and their limitations in this process; and *recognition* that charity has very limited power to overcome social disadvantage.

Put differently, lack of resources and lack of democratic mandate are key weaknesses of foundations, but they are also among their potential core strengths. The key is that foundation resources are 'free' from the constraints of government and market institutions.

Genuinely creative, innovative ideas are in short supply. But endowed foundations, free of market constraints and political considerations, and as yet uncaptured by any single professional or disciplinary group, have the potential to fill this gap. Foundations can, if they choose, think the unthinkable. They can take risks, consider approaches others say can't possibly work—and they can fail with no terminal consequences. Equally important, foundations have the luxury of being able to take a longer-term view. They can be imaginative and creative, working across sectoral, organisational, professional and disciplinary boundaries, without the stifling constraints of short-term and inappropriate performance and measurement criteria. These characteristics give endowed foundations the potential to make a contribution to society out of all proportion to their limited resources.

The creative foundation has several signature elements.

## Personal qualities

Foundations need to work on all stages in the creative process, generating ideas and following through on implementation. Foundations need to ensure a mix of creative qualities among trustees and staff and to make imagination an important recruitment criterion. Foundations need to consider carefully their use of staff and advisers from specialist professional areas and to avoid those who are locked into professional and disciplinary boxes (though such 'specialist' knowledge may have an important role later on in the process); the old polymath advisers often used by earlier foundations may have been more creative.

## Will and leadership

Creativity and innovation require will and leadership—but less in the sense of power than in giving vision and meaning. They require energy and dynamism, discipline and control, concentration and focus, resolve and readiness to take decisions, patience, perseverance and tolerance, initiative and courage, and the capacity to organise, integrate, and synthesise. Foundations need to consider ways in which they can develop these qualities among staff and trustees, and the changes in culture that this requires.

## Human diversity and access to varied talent

Real creativity and innovation require new approaches, new combinations, and a mix of perspectives, cultures and disciplines. They need outsiders to give freshness and all the virtues that go with lack of insider knowledge and first impressions. They need insiders to provide deep knowledge and understanding. If foundations are to be creative and innovative in their own thinking and in their grant-making, they need to find ways of ensuring access to diverse, varied talents and ideas. They need to be able to combine access to deep knowledge and understanding with access to those who can see things in a fresh light unencumbered by preconceptions from the past.

## Organisational culture

Creativity and innovation require particular organisational cultures. The culture needs to positively encourage 'deviant' thinking and working, and expanding possibilities, 'pushing the envelope' or 'out of the box' in the current jargon, and learning within and from outside the organisation. Creative organisations understand the virtues of failure—but they also understand that there is no virtue in failure unless it is analysed and lessons learned. Cultures of creativity recognise the value of catalysts but, because innovation is risky and scary, acknowledge that catalysts need rewards and incentives to become involved.

## Organisational capacity

Good intentions are not enough to make a creative, innovative organisation. Creative organisations need organisational capacities to make creativity work. They need leadership capacity, technical competence, and up-to-date knowledge about what is going on. Foundations are well placed to develop these capacities but they will need changes in culture and practice, time and commitment, and new skills. Crucially, foundations will need to learn to take a longer-term view and to accept that, working alone, they can achieve very little. Working with others, within and across sectors, will require new values, new processes, and new skills.

**Networking and associative structures**

Networking feeds effective creativity and innovation. Wide, deep, and dense networks increase the capacity for ideas and learning not merely because they increase access to existing approaches but also because they increase the likelihood of generating new ideas. Networks are essential to creative effective implementation—in real life very few social issues come in boxes with a single label or 'owner'.

**Next Steps**

Of course, the creative foundation will not come about overnight, and a sustained and systematic effort will be needed to develop the idea more fully and to chart the legal and political implications at the macro level and the economic and organisational implications at the micro level. To this end, we suggest the following open agenda in the hope that others will add to it. We group these agenda items under the three headings of *knowledge*, *basics*, and *correctives*.

**Knowledge**

The creative foundation requires knowledge about the field it works in and about the problems and needs it wants to address and how; and, importantly, it requires knowledge about itself. Some of the critical agenda items are:

- *Research*.   Without more and better research on foundations generally, efforts to develop a platform for the creative foundation will be severely handicapped.  At the very least, without the benefit of a sound knowledge base, the concept of a 'creative foundation' could run the danger of becoming little for than jargon.

- *Information*.   More comprehensive and up-to-date information is needed on foundations generally, and on assets, disbursements, activities funded, organisational structure, boards, and so forth, specifically.

- *Knowledge management*.  New ways and means have to be found to ensure that foundations are in a position to acquire and use knowledge effectively and creatively.  Importantly: how can foundations become learning organisations that share knowledge and understanding of issues with others?

- *Discussion forum* on the future of foundations. This forum would allow a broad and diverse debate about the future of foundations, and enlist the ideas and support of experts as well as outsiders from diverse backgrounds.

- *Task force*.  A task force or working group would be needed to develop the idea of the creative foundation more fully, to look for examples in a systematic way and mine them for insights and so on.

**Basics**

This is, of course, the most challenging part of the process towards the development of a creative foundation. A more comprehensive list will undoubtedly emerge as the work goes forward; we flag only some of the agenda items we regard as most critical here, and formulate them in the form of questions.

- What kind of deed would the creative foundations require? Can we think of 'creative deeds' that allow for both change and continuity? How can protection of the wishes/rights of donors be balanced with flexibility and creativity?

- What external incentive structures are needed for the creative foundation? Are changes required in the current tax treatment of foundation? Should the creative foundation be located within or outside the boundaries of charity law? Could it indeed become one of the areas of innovation anticipated in current government policy thinking that encourages the development of new legal forms for charities (Cabinet Office, 2002)?

- What internal incentives structures best encourage creativity and innovation in foundations? What roles can grant managers and programme officers play in that respect?

- What is the appropriate governance structure for the creative foundations? Will the near-omnipotent role of boards and the near-complete lack of voice of others have to be rethought?

- What are the advantages and disadvantages of creative foundation models that are flexible in terms of longevity? There is a need to rethink exit options for funders and foundations, and to explore other time-limited models such as project funds.

- Should the creative foundation step over conventional distinctions such as grant-making vs. operating foundations or membership-based versus non-membership based organisations, and try out new forms and combinations?

- Should the creative foundation establish itself as a separate entity, set apart from conventional foundations? The 20th-century foundation differentiated itself from the19th-century charity. What would be the 21st-century equivalent?

## Correctives

Even though models for creative foundation will take time for development, discussion and 'testing', policy-makers and the foundation community can take some steps now. As before, we list them on the understanding that a more complete catalogue of 'things to do' will be drawn up in the future:

- diversify board composition and invite trustees to join for specific time periods only;

- move away from an emphasis of funding organisations and consider funding individuals;

- put less emphasis on performance and impact measurement; instead, 'front-load' the grant-making process and take risks;

- concentrate on fuller assessments of grants impacts that stress learning over control; and

- strengthen the infrastructure for foundations locally, nationally, and internationally in terms of umbrella organisations and lobbying groups.

# Conclusion

Endowed foundations are not, never can be, and never should be substitutes for government and statutory provision. They have neither the resources nor the democratic mandate to take on these roles. Nevertheless, endowed foundations have never been more important than they are today. Most societies are increasingly dominated by short-term market considerations and the values of competition and individualism. Foundations offer alternative, wider and longer-term viewpoints. They have the space and the resources to stand back and question the mantras of the day and to encourage truly creative thinking to address the issues into which they, and others, have poured vast amounts of money, so far with little lasting effect.

Yet, as we embark on developing new visions, roles, and models for foundations, it is important to admit openly that perhaps too many foundations have lost their way. Old roles and philosophies, if they ever were viable, provide little direction in today's environment. The crisis of confidence in the foundation world does not stem from a lack of resources. The roots of the crisis of philanthropy lie in lack of any clear articulation of coherent vision for foundations, and a lack of sustainable roles that play to their strengths rather than to their weaknesses. Foundations are neither poor imitations of government nor the chosen tools for venture philanthropists in search of quick fixes. They are something far more important: They are the potential powerhouses of creative thinking and working that modern society needs.

In conclusion, we suggest four immediate challenges that have to be approached if the agenda proposed here is to move forward. The first two challenges are specifically addressed to foundation representatives and philanthropists, while the latter two call primarily upon policy-makers.

**Challenge 1: promote a culture of innovation and creativity**

- Review induction and training procedures for trustees and foundation staff in terms of innovative thinking.

- Identify exemplary cases of innovation and creativity and best practices; show where innovation and creativity made a difference.

- Establish new forums to encourage innovation in the foundation world and for rewarding creative grant-making.

**Challenge 2: strengthen diffusion of knowledge and encourage learning**

- Develop and establish governance models that treat innovation as process, not as some end product that can be measured with conventional performance indicators.

- Provide incentives for information-sharing about innovative and creative grant-making among foundation staff.

- Support cooperative ventures among foundations, and 'cluster approaches' to creative problem-solving.

- Review the role of umbrella organisations for grant-making foundations.

**Challenge 3: place innovation capacity at the centre of regulatory reforms**

- Review the adequacy of current legal frameworks for foundations, in particular the notions of charity, public benefit, deed, and trusteeship. Specifically, we encourage foundations to examine the proposals made by the Cabinet's Office Strategy Unit Report (2002).

- Review the role of the Charity Commission, and the need for a separate supervisory body or branch of the Commission for grant-making institutions.

- Review the impact of globalisation and European Union policy-making on UK philanthropy, and the implications for the current legal framework for foundations.

**Challenge 4: Increase the number of medium-sized and large foundations, and encourage smaller endowments to explore new forms of philanthropic institutions, particularly donor-advised funds and other vehicles of individual engagement for public benefit outside conventional forms.**

- Target potential founders of small to medium-sized foundations and encourage them to set up innovative, creative institutions.

- Encourage smaller foundations to experiment with new forms, board structures, and grantee relationships.

- Put in place procedures and incentive systems that encourage established foundations to reorganise and transform themselves into more innovative institutions.

# Chapter 1

# Opening Up Debate

# Introduction

This report seeks to open up debate about the proper roles of philanthropic foundations in modern democratic society. The present report is, however, not a conventional research account. It is a combination of evidence, hypothesis, exhortation, and even speculation. Where possible we have drawn on empirical evidence, but the available research on British foundations is simply insufficient to provide a solid, systematic picture of what foundations in this country do, how they operate, for what purpose, and to what effect. As we argue below, more research is urgently needed, not least to support or refute our claims. Much of the foundation literature is normative, telling us what foundations aspire to – often in a way that suggests this is what they actually do.

There is a need to challenge the conventional myths on which much of current foundation legitimacy is based. We want to encourage foundations to become more reflective and open about what they do, how, and for what wider purpose. Our aim is not only to encourage research into these questions, but also to provide a new and more robust justification for the continued role and importance of foundations in a modern democracy. Some may agree with our argument; others may not. That is all to the good, and part of the wider debate we wish to ignite in the hope that other foundations will take up the gauntlet and fund both further debate and research on the issues raised in this report.

In this report, we focus on foundations, rather than charities in general, not because they have any special legal status (they do not) but because endowed foundations are freer than charities without an independent, secure income to fulfil the creative roles we believe are urgently needed in modern society. We also think that a special look of foundations is warranted in the light of recent reports like the Cabinet's Strategy Unit (2002) that looked at the modernisation of Britain's charities and voluntary sector but with limited attention paid to foundations and trusts specifically.

In line with statements in the Cabinet Office's *Review* of the voluntary sector (2002: 32), we suggest that charities more generally, and foundations specifically, are vitally important institutions for advanced countries like Britain, but we also argue that in particular foundations are some way from fulfilling this promise. We believe that foundations are especially relevant in the current political climate that puts less emphasis on governmental responsibilities and actions and allocates more 'space' to private institutions serving the public good. Yet some of the evidence we review in this report casts serious doubt upon whether foundations with their current forms and practices have the potential to meet the sometimes-lofty expectations invested in them.

At worst, foundations are little more than tax shelters for the privileged to pursue some favoured cause or charity; at best, foundations are engines of social innovation and a vital support for creativity in modern societies. Foundations are too important to be allowed to fall short of their potential. These may be strong assertions, we know, and we could easily point to good and bad examples of foundation practices: of course, some foundations not only benefit the poor but also enable them to overcome poverty; other foundations support research and education or help the handicapped and the elderly. These foundations add to the common good, and serve a useful purpose, even though we ultimately may not be able to specify precisely how much and relative to what other way or form.

By contrast, other foundations serve the privileged few, with no apparent net benefit to society as a whole.  Others use their endowments less to support some specified cause, however beneficial, esoteric, or necessary it might be, than to safeguard and add to fortunes already in place. Still others do very little at all, hold ritualistic board meetings, and resemble rather passive, even docile institutions seemingly at odds with the faster pace of the 21st century.

Yet, from a policy perspective, these contrasting caricatures are part of the problem we face when trying to assess foundations: beyond some basic facts and figures, the empirical information about them is patchy, largely unsystematic, and incomplete.  Indeed, one of the most striking and firm conclusions one can draw about philanthropic foundations is that we know remarkably little about them.  They are *terra incognita*, and from a research perspective we should exercise caution and not assume a priori that foundations can live up to the political expectations invested in them as instruments of social reform.

Why have foundations been neglected as a field of policy analysis and academic study for so long?  There are several reasons why it is easy to overlook foundations: politically, they are rarely put under the same scrutiny as governments and public agencies that face elections and a watchful press; economically, they are more sheltered than other private institutions from changing market fortunes and pressures from shareholders; and culturally, they are protected by a subtle consensus that discourages a critique of institutions that are regarded as inherently 'good' and serving the public interest. This neglect has become something of a protective shield that safeguards foundations from critical, constructive debate—a shield we intend to remove in this report.

We do so not in the spirit of criticism for criticism's sake. We are supporters of foundations and philanthropy (and, of course, they support us!), and we defend the need of societies to allow, and encourage, independent private action for public benefit. We believe that foundations ultimately add to modern societies' problem-solving capacity whether in the field of education, health, culture, or policy development, among others. The freedom foundations have from both ballot box and shareholder expectations affords them great latitude in pursuing private objectives and agendas while serving a public purpose. Yet, as we will point out, few foundations take full advantage of this freedom, and, for reasons which we will identify, many are not realising their full potential and the great promise they hold for modern societies like Britain.

There is, we suggest, a significant hiatus between the promise and the reality of foundations, a hiatus that stands in marked contrast to the renewed interest in philanthropic foundations not only in Britain but also in countries as different as the United States, Japan, Italy, Germany, Sweden, Turkey, and Brazil. By the early 1980s, observers had begun to note a reversal in the decline in the overall size and importance of the foundation sector that characterised the previous two decades, which itself followed a prolonged period of relative stagnation (see Anheier and Toepler 1999a for an overview). As part of a general reappraisal of the role of the state in modern society (Salamon and Anheier 1996), however, foundations were discovered and rediscovered by policy-makers, and throughout the 1990s and into the early years of the 21st century foundations have experienced, and continue to experience, a significant renaissance.

With the number of foundations increasing (see Leat 2001; Vincent and Pharoah 2000 for the UK; Anheier 2001 for Europe; Renz 2002, for the US), it would seem that the 'golden age' of philanthropy neither began nor ended when the big foundations were established by Rowntree, Nuffield, Rockefeller, and Ford. It would be more accurate to link at least the potential for a 'golden age' to present times. Within little more than two decades, foundations in many countries have passed from a period of relative decline and irrelevance to a phase of unprecedented growth and increasing policy importance. For example, over half of the foundations in Britain were created after 1970 (Villemur 1995: ix; Leat 2001: 278). Thus, at least in terms of numbers, foundations not just in Britain but also in the United States, Germany, Italy, the Netherlands, Canada, Spain, Australia and other countries represent essentially a late 20th-century phenomenon.

## The Problem

Against this growth and the heightened expectations philanthropy enjoys in the current political environment, it is important for both policy-makers and practitioners to explore the real potential of foundations and other philanthropic institutions. Therefore, this report poses fundamental questions: why do modern societies need philanthropic foundations in the first place? What case, if any, could be made for the continuation of foundations in their present state? What is the potential for the renewal and reform of philanthropy? Is the so-called 'new philanthropy' any different from the old?

Even though most British foundations have been created in the latter part of the 20th century (see above; Leat 2001: 271), the form of the philanthropic foundation as it exists today is largely a late 19th-century creation. As an institution, the philanthropic foundation reflected the social responsibilities and moral obligations of the large fortunes made during the industrial revolution at a time when the powers of the state to tax and regulate were comparatively underdeveloped (see Smith and Borgmann 2001). Today, however, we look at philanthropy in the context of a retreating state (privatisation of the public sector, often by stealth, as with higher education, social services, culture and the arts, and health), corporate responsibility, and the 'new money' of the 1990s linked to information technologies, and the globalisation of financial and other markets.

Philanthropy, however, underwent its last real modernisation in the early part of the 20th century when the introduction of the large-scale US foundations (Carnegie, Ford) spilled over to Britain. Since then philanthropy has become largely synonymous with grant-making foundations and charitable trusts, and the philanthropist synonymous with rich donors of individual largesse. Widespread innovations in organised philanthropy have been rare and only in recent years have new forms such as venture philanthropy begun to emerge (Emerson and Twersky, 1996, 199x; Letts, Ryan, and Grossman 1997; Reis and

Clohsey 2001; Breiteneicher and Marble 2001).[1] Of course, many successful and well-functioning foundations exist, but we wonder whether those that are not outnumber them. Unfortunately, the evidence that would allow us to answer that question is patchy and unsystematic.

Many larger, well-established foundations developed into bureaucratic organisations that make grants in highly organised and professional ways. They resemble quasi-aristocratic institutions with their wide autonomy in making decisions about fund distribution and the near-complete lack of recourse on the part of rejected grant-seekers. In fact, foundations may well be the modern social institution that affords the least 'voice' to those seeking support. For smaller foundations we find a different pattern. They are well-meaning but frequently ineffective, and run by cautious trustees who serve in a voluntary capacity. These trustees tend to favour stability and orderly accounts over innovation and risk-taking, which may ultimately reduce effectiveness and impact. Indeed, liability requirements and other legal aspects of the trusteeship system encourage prudence but also caution and risk-aversion.

Even though UK foundations have seen their assets increase in recent years (Pharoah 2001), they play minor roles in financing public services in education, health, social services, arts and culture, the environment, international development, and humanitarian assistance—in most cases less than 1–2 per cent of total expenditure in the field (Kendall and Almond 1998). Even though they could react more quickly than public agencies to special problems and unforeseen circumstances, most do not; and many larger foundations have become bureaucratic and inert

---

[1] See also the International Network on Strategic Philanthropy (URL).

over time, while smaller ones are frequently idiosyncratic and unpredictable. Moreover, smaller foundations yield below-market returns on assets (Salamon 1992; Porter and Kramer 1999), and arguably they are little more than 'dead-hand' properties permanently excluded from economic circulation in markets where they could very likely yield greater returns, both private and public.

Yet we suggest that it is not here that the critical problem of organised philanthropy lies. True, philanthropy all too often developed into a genteel, seemingly academic world of social reformers, supporters of high culture, and gap-fillers of welfare state functions. It was, and in many ways still is, a world at peace with itself and its frequently self-ascribed importance. As we will show in Chapter 3, the boards of foundations more or less reflect a country's elite and not its innovative potential for the future. Again, this is a criticism going back to the beginnings of the modern foundation over 100 years ago, and similar critiques have been voiced from across the political spectrum (see for example Boulding 1962; Nielsen 1979; Arnove 1980; Odendahl 1987a, b; Prewitt 1999). We could add many other such critiques to show that philanthropy is less than a perfect institution.

*The true problem, however, lies elsewhere: it is simply that the world around philanthropy has changed, while philanthropy has not, holding on to the models, practices, and culture of the past.*

Let's be open: were it not for the reappraisal of the role of state and the increased prosperity and inequality of British society, and were it not for the pressing search of institutional alternatives to the 'welfare state' in addressing the social challenges of our times, little would have to be said about philanthropy today. We have to reassess philanthropy not so much because of the easy promise it might entail, but because other mechanisms (taxation, state action, private markets) are increasingly becoming (or are believed to be) inefficient and ineffective in a variety of fields ranging from social services and health to education and culture.

Part of the problem is a reluctance to be frank and open about institutions that appear inherently good, at least at first glance. Yet it is now of paramount importance for policy-makers, and not only a matter of academic discourse, to ask: what in the institution of philanthropy is worth preserving, developing, even nurturing? By implication, are there other elements that are best left by the wayside or actively discontinued? What is the true potential of philanthropy for the future of British and other developed societies—societies that are becoming less egalitarian, less state-oriented, and less stable, but more mobile and individualistic, and with greater institutional uncertainties and higher risks?

The best empirical case that analysts have been able to make for foundations appears sobering at first: foundations are primarily important to ensure institutional diversity in funding, and to counteract monopolistic tendencies of both state and market. They can introduce and nurture new ideas outside the arena of government policy and party politics, and promote agendas shielded from market forces. Yet how can foundations maintain such a role in the future? And could not more be achieved, given the potential and growth of private fortunes?

These questions are particularly timely in the current policy environment, which casts philanthropy in a positive and proactive role (Brown 2000; Cabinet Office, 2002).  As in many other countries, changing ideas about the role of the state in meeting the social, educational, cultural, and environmental challenges of modern societies have brought private voluntary action and philanthropy closer to the centre stage of current policy debates in Britain.  In consultation with voluntary sector organisations and philanthropic institutions, the Labour Government has launched a major policy initiative to support the development of an active and local 'civic society' (Brown 2000; Plowden 2001; Deakin 2001; Cabinet Office, 2002).

Central to this initiative are both the introduction of wide-ranging incentives to increase philanthropic giving, and second a proposed legal reform based on a modernisation of charity law and legal forms available to voluntary sector organisations. To a large extent, the Conservative Party largely endorses both policy initiatives as well.  Through tax incentives and other measures, these reforms aim to encourage the voluntary giving of money, shares, stocks, and other property at levels unprecedented in this and other major countries, including the United States.

Importantly, however, these reforms were initiated without examining the actual potential of philanthropy, and foundations in particular, to live up to the promise held out by the government.  Does Britain have the right kind of philanthropy to go with the current tax proposals and other changes in charity law and voluntary sector policies?  Can philanthropy meet current challenges and opportunities?  Is the tax relief and other privileges granted to philanthropy worth it: that is, does society gain more from foundations and other philanthropic activities than it might from greater taxation and scrutiny of private wealth? And, if not, what changes are needed?

Clearly, the world around foundations is changing. Perhaps as little as 20 years ago their roles were relatively clear and generally agreed. Now those roles are less easy to defend. Foundations need a new philosophy adapted to the changes in the world around them. Without a new, clearly articulated vision, foundations are in danger of having inappropriate roles and expectations thrust upon them. Without such a modern vision, foundations are unlikely to be able to inspire the next generation of philanthropists, and the willingness of future policy-makers to extent tax and other privileges to foundations.

## Nagging Questions

The report begins by questioning the *raison d'être* and role of philanthropic foundations in today's society, and poses fundamental questions about their existence and performance. The discussion is deliberately provocative and designed to challenge current thinking about foundations. We identify issues, pose claims and counter-claims, and develop arguments 'pro' and 'con'. Where possible we draw on UK research and commentary to substantiate our points, but this literature is sparse (which we take as an indication of the serious lack of public and academic interest in foundations in this country). Indeed, we find that in the UK, unlike the US, charitable foundations are rarely publicly discussed and even more rarely criticised. Therefore, when relevant to the UK situation, we make use of the more voluminous US literature to make points and parallels, and also incorporate material from other countries and regions, primarily Europe and Australia.

We argue that foundations have in important ways played to their weaknesses rather than their strengths. Foundations have been over-ambitious, over-claiming, and, at the same time, even somewhat over-apologetic. In the final chapter we suggest a new vision for foundations and discuss some of the organisational and cultural characteristics that foundations would need to display in order to realise this vision.

Our focus is on charitable or philanthropic foundations in Britain, irrespective of whether they are registered as charities. In the UK the terms 'charity' and 'philanthropy' are often used interchangeably. In the US, however, they refer to different activities; 'charity' means giving for the relief of symptoms whereas 'philanthropy' is reserved for giving that addresses causes. By contrast, in the UK philanthropy has become more synonymous with charitable foundations and trusts, and being a philanthropist synonymous with the largesse of rich individual donors. With the term 'philanthropy' usually reserved for larger donations, it carries with it undertones of elitism and reflections of the British class structure stemming from the Victorian era (see Lewis 1999). To exaggerate somewhat, the popular British view is that the rich practise philanthropy while the poor give to charity.

The charity-philanthropy distinction reflects the divergent development of philanthropy in both the US and the UK since the early 20th century. While in the US the modern, methodical, and self-confident approach of the large-scale US foundations (Carnegie, Rockefeller, Ford, Mott) replaced Victorian models and ideals of philanthropy (see Karl and Katz 1981), very little such modernising replacement took place in Britain. What is more, no 'indigenous' version of 20th-century philanthropy challenged the Victorian model in a significant way, although some institutional transfer from the US to Britain has occurred, particularly since 1945.

However, such imports did little to change the identity of charity and philanthropy in their intent and objective. The separation that occurred in the US nearly100 years ago has yet to develop and take effect in Britain, even though some foundations have long addressed underlying social issues. This includes the J. Rowntree Foundation on poverty and social inequality, the Cadbury support of the Runnymead Trust's work on racism in Britain, foundation support for integrated education in Northern Ireland, or funding for women's refuge centres. In all these cases, foundations made a difference, and their moved public debate forward in a critical way. Yet we ask: why do we see not more of such initiatives among the nearly 10,000 foundations in this country?

Indeed, over the last century, surprisingly few innovations originated and took hold in the world of UK foundations and trusts given the significant freedom the institutions enjoy. The most notable exception is venture philanthropy, itself a US import, which has begun to emerge in recent years, often spearheaded by financiers with American background and experience, e.g., individual philanthropists like Peter Lample who addresses educational inequalities, or funder circles as in the case of Shine, a trust devoted to educational reform in England.

The general lack of innovation raises a fundamental question: from what base and against what model can the modernisation of British philanthropy proceed? The task of finding a place for philanthropy in 21st-century Britain is complicated by the absence of 20th-century developments to modernise and replace Victorian models and practices, both among foundations and potential donors, and among the population at large. As a result, the public perception of foundations often draws a blank and is curiously caught up in past models, if at all, and not in present practices. What is more, scholarly attention, in particular policy analysis, has largely neglected the cultural-institutional hiatus in which UK foundations and philanthropic practices find themselves due to the long-term absence of modernisation.

Thus, the convenient distinction between charity and philanthropy in tracing the long-term development of the US model for foundations does not apply to the UK. In the US, the trajectory moves from the relief of symptoms to the direct elimination of causes and, increasingly, to the creation of enabling conditions for social, cultural and political innovation (see Stanfield 1995). Behind this trajectory are long-standing public and academic debates about the role and usefulness of foundations in American society, however ideological and politically biased they might appear to British audiences. But no such debates have taken place in Britain, at least in recent decades.

What is more, whereas the voluntary and community sector in Britain have become the subject of keen policy interest (for example, the Compact, the Active Community Unit, the Policy Innovation Unit in the Cabinet Office, the Treasury) such attention has largely bypassed foundations (see Plowden 2001; Leat 2001). While analysts have had much to say about the role and potential of voluntary organisations, either as service providers or advocates, foundations have found little mention, and have certainly not been seen as a central policy issue.

Likewise, the Campaign for Giving, launched in 2000 by the Labour Government to promote the new tax law relating to charitable donations, aimed at increasing giving to charities, yet put hardly any emphasis on encouraging the creation of foundations. Thus, any assessment of the potential of foundations in this country cannot pick up existing strands of debate or current policies. Instead, it must start with the 'basics' and examine a wide range of issues and questions, which we have grouped into four related 'issue clusters'. These clusters will serve as the initial moorings for our discussion.

1. Why do foundations exist in the first place? What theoretical and empirical arguments can be made for and against their existence? Why do foundations continue to exist, and what would be the effect of their abolition?

2. If, as they claim, foundations have a major role in promoting innovation, are they, as currently constituted, equipped to play this role? What are the sources of innovation of innovation and renewal in foundations?

3. What are the key changes in their wider environment in recent years, and how have foundations and new forms of philanthropy responded to these developments?

4. What is the present and future role of foundations in Britain? How could foundations give real meaning to their aspirations to be innovative, creative organisations?

Before we can explore these questions, we need to address a few definitional issues, in large measure because the term 'foundation' tends to be used in a rather loose and imprecise way.

## Defining Foundations

This report focuses on organised philanthropy in the form of foundations. This poses the immediate question of what kind of foundation we have in mind. Even a cursory look at the UK, other European countries, and the US reveals a rich tapestry of philanthropic institutions and a great variety of forms. Thus, one of our first tasks is to bring some conceptual clarity and focus to the subject, and to indicate which types of foundation we have in mind and which are outside our primary interest. For the purposes of this report, we follow the structural-operational definition of non-profit organisations proposed by Salamon and Anheier (1997) and define a foundation as an asset, financial or otherwise, with the following characteristics:

*Non-membership-based organisation*. The foundation must rest on an original deed, typically signified in a charter of incorporation or establishment that gives the entity both purpose and relative permanence. Other aspects include some degree of internal organisational structure, relative persistence of goals, structure, and activities, and meaningful organisational boundaries. Thus, a foundation is not only a financial or other type of asset but also an identifiable organisation.

*Private entity*. Foundations are institutionally separate from government, and are 'non-governmental' in the sense of not being instrumentalities of government. Therefore, foundations do not exercise governmental authority and are outside direct majoritarian control.

*Self-governing entity*. Foundations are equipped to control their own activities, have their own internal governance procedures, enjoy a meaningful degree of autonomy, and have a separate set of accounts in the sense that assets, expenditures, and other disbursements must not be part of either governmental of corporate balance sheets.

*Non-profit-distributing entity*. Foundations do not return profits to their trustees or directors generated by either use of assets or the conduct of commercial activities. A foundation may accumulate a surplus in a given year, but the surplus must be applied to its basic mission and not be distributed to owners or their equivalents.

*Serving a public purpose*. Foundations should do more than serve the needs of a narrowly defined social group or category, such as members of a family or a closed circle of beneficiaries. Foundations are private assets that serve a public purpose. The public purpose may or may not be charitable and therefore tax-exempt in the letter or spirit of charity law. What is important is that the purpose be part of the public domain.

The terms 'foundation' or 'trust' are usually used to refer to organisations that have an endowment from which they derive income. However, some foundations do not have a permanent endowment. Some may, for example, derive their income from a regular covenant (for example, some company foundations), and other types like community foundations may have an endowment but also raise money for current expenditure and for building up their asset base.  Other foundations may have little or no endowment, and raise money annually, but behave in many important respects much like endowed foundations (for example, BBC Children-in-Need and the Community Fund). In this report, we are primarily concerned with endowed foundations, but we make reference to other types.

## Foundations in England and Wales[2]

There are over 9,000 charitable foundations in England and Wales, and a much smaller but unknown number of foundations that give grants for public benefit but are not registered as charities (in part because this would restrict their range of activities). It is estimated that UK trusts and foundations give about £2 billion in grants each year. In addition around £280 million is given by a small number of large operating charities that give grants in the course of their work (for example, Oxfam). The total sum given by trusts and foundations is about the same as the total of grants (as distinct from contracts) given to charities by government. While total trust funding is only a small part of total voluntary sector income, it is especially important in that it is unconstrained by either market or political considerations (Kendall and Knapp 1996; Kendall and Almond 1998).

Foundations differ radically in their resources, staffing, structures, purposes, and activities. Assets, income, and grant disbursements are very unevenly spread among foundations, thus concentrating the major powers of grant-making in a very few hands. Around 90 per cent of total income and grant disbursements are represented by about 10 per cent of foundations. In the UK a small number of foundations are well-endowed, employ professional staff, give grants according to some strategic plan, and so on. By contrast, the vast majority have small assets, give few if any grants each year, employ no staff, and give grants seemingly at random in response to requests received or according to the whim of those controlling resources. It is important to be aware of the dangers of generalising from the small number of larger foundations, about which most is known. However, although these larger foundations are unrepresentative of foundations in general, they do command the vast majority of assets and income and are thus, in a sense, the most important (on foundations in the UK see also Siederer 1996; Fitzherbert and Richards 2001).

## Foundation Types

There are two basic ways in which foundations can achieve their purpose: by engaging third parties (grantees, contractors, and so on) or by performing the tasks themselves. Some foundations conduct both activities. We can group British foundations by type of activity and type of founder.

---

[2] See Leat (2001), Pharoah and Siederer (1997), and Vincent and Pharoah (2000) for information cited in this section unless indicated otherwise.

**Type of activity**

*Grant-making foundations*: endowed organisations that primarily engage in grant making for specified purposes. Examples range from the wealthy and well-known such as The Leverhulme Trust and the Nuffield Foundation to the much less wealthy and lesser known such as Sir Siegmund Warburg's Voluntary Settlement.

*Operating foundations*: organisations with some form of endowment that primarily operate their own programmes and projects (but may also engage in some grant-making). Examples include Charities Aid Foundation and the Charities Advisory Trust.

*Mixed foundations*: foundations which operate their own programs and projects and engage in grant-making on a significant scale. Examples include Joseph Rowntree Foundation and the Kings Fund.

The definition proposed above emphasises the crucial role founders play in setting up foundations. They provide the original deed, and thereby link the donated assets to specific purposes. Clearly, the type of founder will have a significant impact on the purpose and operations of foundations.

**Type of founder**

*Individual*: foundations founded by an individual, group of individuals or family whereby donors bring their private assets into the foundation. The nature of the assets can be stock and other shares in business firms, financial, real estate, patents, and so on.

*Corporate foundations* come in several subtypes. The most prominent type is the company-related or company-sponsored foundation. Corporate foundations vary in the extent to which they maintain close links to the parent corporations in terms of governance and management. Examples include Lloyds TSB Foundations and Allied Dunbar Foundation.

*Community foundations*: grant-making organisations that pool revenue and assets from a variety of sources (individual, corporate, public) for specified communal purposes. Examples include the Isle of Dogs Community Foundation and The Community Foundation in Wales.

*Government-sponsored or government-created foundations*: foundations that fit the definition but are either created by public charter or enjoy high degrees of public sector support for either endowment or operating expenditures. Examples include the Westminster Foundation for Democracy, and the Northern Ireland Voluntary Trust.

Table 1 classifies foundations by founder/instigator/key source of endowment and basic form, and illustrates in broad terms the diversity of foundations in the United Kingdom, ranging from grant-making foundations established by individuals to corporate foundations and government creations. Individuals create most foundations in Britain. It is unclear whether governments are making more or less use of foundations, even though government-inspired grant-making bodies have become prominent in recent years as exemplified by the Lottery Boards (see FitzHerbert, Addison, Rahman 1999). For corporations, data in Britain suggest the opposite trend (Smyth, 2000; Logan, 2002).

In this report, we primarily focus on endowed grant-making foundations created by individuals. We make only passing reference to operating foundations and mixed types, developments in the world of corporate foundations, and foundations created by government; these other types of foundation deserve more detailed consideration in further work. We have chosen to focus on foundations created by individuals because these form the bulk of foundations in Britain and because they highlight most clearly the key dilemmas for and the potential of foundations.

**Table 1: Major Types of Foundations in the United Kingdom**

| Instigator/Founder or key source of endowment | Primary focus | | |
| | Grant-making | Operating | Mixed |
| --- | --- | --- | --- |
| Private individual(s) | Nuffield Foundation | | Nuffield Foundation |
| Corporation(s) | Allied Dunbar | The Fishmongers' Company's Charitable Trust | Camelot Foundation |
| Government | Community Fund, Children Fund | The Family Fund<br><br>Coal Field Regeneration Trust | Westminster Foundation for Democracy |
| Mixed sources | Charity Know How (now Allavida)<br><br>Arts Council | Mental Health Foundation | Charities Aid Foundation;<br><br>Community foundations |

# Core Dilemmas

Foundations face a number of core dilemmas in relation to their strategic direction, operations, and external relations. Although all foundations share these dilemmas, they are more or less acute depending on the type of foundation. The themes of control, risk, independence, and privacy run through these dilemmas. The dilemmas or tensions are outlined here under the three headings of strategy, operations, and relations, although in practice some dilemmas straddle these headings. They are best appreciated with the help of a thought experiment. Assuming one had £1 billion in financial assets available to put toward some identifiable public benefit, how would one go about it? Here are some of the key issues that would need to be addressed:

## Strategic dilemmas

- Focusing on the alleviation of symptoms vs. understanding their causes and aiming for structural reform and policy change.

- Maintaining independence of government vs. working with government to achieve lasting change and greater leverage, or subsidising state activities.

- Allowing maximum donor control vs. responding to pressing needs and demand.

- Remaining true to the founder's formal preferences and informal intentions vs. responding to change and opportunities for innovation.

- Balancing professionalisation and bureaucratisation of grant-making with space for innovation and 'out-of-the-box' thinking.

- Balancing responsible stewardship of funds with the real risk-taking most innovations involve.

- Maximising foundation income and asset building vs. remaining true to principles and mission

- Maximising income for grant-making vs. spending on infrastructure, salaries and organisational capacity.

**Operational dilemmas**

- Funding those applicants with a reputation and proven track record vs. funding the new and the untried.

- Funding those applicants known to the foundation vs. equal chances for all applicants

- Regular monitoring of grant recipients vs. allowing flexibility of grant recipients to respond to changing circumstances.

- Funding only those applicants with the capacity for sustainability vs. taking chances on change.

- Responding to open applications vs. proactively choosing priorities.

- Small number of large grants for maximum impact vs. larger number of small grants for maximum spread.

- Giving longer-term grants (silting up) vs. retaining flexibility via shorter-term grants.

- Funding core costs vs. project costs with an obvious time limit.

- Giving applicants all they ask for (encouraging dependence) vs. funding for failure (too little for too short a time).

- Ensuring knowledge and continuity among trustees and staff vs. introducing change and risking discontinuity and loss of institutional knowledge.

- Sticking to set operational principles vs. changing the way in which the foundations reaches its goals (from grant-making to mixed or operating foundation; running own project vs. having third parties carry them out.

## Relational dilemmas

- Working with other funders (including other foundations) vs. maintaining independence and encouraging diversity and pluralism.

- Maximising the independence of grantees vs. ensuring control to secure maximum outcome value of foundation grant.

- Publicising existence and work vs. fears of overload, raising expectations, and so on.

- Maintaining privacy to allow freedom to fund unpopular causes and so forth vs. maximising transparency and accountability.

These core dilemmas run through much of the discussion in the following chapters. These issues present themselves throughout the organisational life cycle of foundations, and perhaps more so once foundations have become established and settled into an operating routine. But underlying these dilemmas are some of the more fundamental questions, which we will address in Chapter 2 when we address the purposes foundations serve and the roles they play.

**Cautionary Note**

We are aware of the speculative nature of some of the points raised in this and the following chapters. In some ways, as one of our reviewers remarked, this report sits somewhat uncomfortably between critical diagnosis and speculation. The latter is, of course, no substitute for systematic data, which unfortunately at present do not exist. More resources for research on philanthropy are urgently needed, which is just one of the suggestions made in the final chapters for ways of carrying forward the lively, constructive debate we hope to provoke.

# Chapter 2

# Why Do Foundations Exist?
# Roles and Rationales

# Introduction

The origins of foundations are disputed, and the answers, ranging from antiquity to the 19th century, depend partly on the definition and geographical focus employed. Smith and Borgman (2001) identify two prominent roots in the development of foundations in Europe: religion, in particular the Roman Catholic and the Protestant Churches, and the 'bourgeois' revolution of the 19th century, when the emerging urban middle class and industrial elite made frequent use of the foundation form. In Britain, the Victorian era saw the first modern 'foundation boom' and a prominent social and political role for organised philanthropy (Prochaska 1990).

The true locus of modern foundation development, however, has been the United States, despite the creation of trusts like the Nuffield and Rowntree foundations in Britain, or the Robert Bosch Foundation in Germany. The initial growth period of foundations in the US reflected the perceived social responsibilities and moral obligations of the entrepreneurs during the post-bellum reconstruction period and the rapid industrialisation that followed. Importantly, in the US foundations represented an innovation that implied a fundamental shift in their *raison d'être*: foundations become problem-solving institutions (see Karl and Katz 1981; Bremner 1956; 1980): Some scholars like Bulmer (1999) see the modern foundation as a prime tool and exemplar of 'knowledge-based social engineering' in modern society. By contrast, in Britain philanthropic institutions largely remained expressions of charity and special interests, closely tied to the industrial class system.

The remarkable achievement of 20th-century US philanthropy was to modernise a basically European institution that had been discredited twice. First, in the aftermath of the French revolution, foundations were seen as an expression of the *'ancien regime'*. Fears of the *'main mort'* dictating the future, and the identification of foundations as bastions of the Church and the aristocracy, paved the way for restrictive laws on foundations in many countries. Foundations survived, of course, were to be 'reborn' as charitable institutions, and reached new prominence in the late 19th century. Foundations became the charitable arm of the new industrial elite, and were fully part of the Victorian model of a self-organising society (see Lewis 1999) with limited state involvement. The workers' movement and the socialist party challenged this model politically, in turn.

In the UK, in all but perhaps the last decade of the 20th century, organised philanthropy appears largely to have followed the model of charitable institutions for specific or general ills (health, social care, poverty, and so on) rather than the problem-solving model adopted by the large US foundations. Other than in the field of medical research, very few British foundations were created to address the causes of problems or explicitly to address policy issue. It is worth noting that only 48 of the top 300 foundations listed in the *Guide to the Major Trusts* (Directory of Social Change 2001/2002) cite policy issues among their interests; there is no separate heading for social research, and only 3 per cent of all grants are estimated to go to 'civil society/law/advocacy' causes (Vincent and Pharoah 2000).[3]

---

[3] In part, these figures may reflect the way in which grants are categorised, but that is another illustration of the need for more, and more sensitive, research.

# Why Foundations?

Irrespective of their historical development as charitable institutions, and irrespective of the missed modernisation push of British philanthropy in the 20th century, we have to ask the fundamental question of why foundations exist in the first place. What theoretical and empirical arguments can be made for and against their existence in the 21st century? We explore these questions by posing two opposing answers, first generally and then from the perspectives of founders, government, and civil society at large.

*Claim: Foundations exist because they lever private money for public benefits and thereby provide additional options to state/market provisions.* Specifically:

- *For founders*: as a form, foundations respond to existing demand, and provide (actual and potential) philanthropists with a legal instrument for expressing and pursuing their philanthropic interests.

- *For government*: foundations provide additional resources (funds, expertise, direct services, and so on) that supplement government action, thereby achieving a more optimal use of both public and private funds.

- *For civil society*: foundations are an independent source of funding that helps civil society counterbalance the forces of markets and state, preventing both from dominating and atomising the rest of society.

**Counterclaim**: *Foundations may have some useful features but they are ultimately elitist, undemocratic, and basically irrelevant to modern society. The privileges they receive and reinforce may well surpass the wider benefits they create.*

- *For founders*: foundations exist to provide a solution to the problems of the rich rather than the poor.

- *For government*: foundations interfere with democratic processes and suck wealth out of the nation's tax base; they represent a misallocation of public funds.

- *For civil society*: foundations continue to exist not because there is evidence that they do anything valuable or that they command widespread support, but because of ignorance, lack of political will and interest, and belief in foundations' myths about themselves.

To put claim and counterclaim into perspective, it is useful to take a closer look at some of the theoretical thinking about foundations.

## Explaining Foundations

Unfortunately, with a few notable exceptions (Boulding 1962; 1972; 1973; Porter and Kramer 1999) economists have traditionally taken little interest in foundations. Sociologists, political scientists, and historians have had more, but not that much, to say about the existence of foundations. One very general theory of the existence of foundations is that they provide vehicles for the expression of individual altruism and the means of leveraging private money for public purposes. On the assumptions of varying levels of philanthropic values and of an unequal distribution of assets in a population, some people will have both high assets and high philanthropic values. For a minority of them, in particular for those with larger fortunes, setting up a foundation for the distribution of grants (or for providing a service) will be economically efficient. In other words, it may be cheaper and less demanding to disburse money for a dedicated purpose with the help of a dedicated organisation, that is, a foundation, than through the agency of the individual founder alone.

Many of the explanations of foundations' existence at the broader societal or cultural level are derived from the US, and, given the very different attitudes to the proper role of the state, are of questionable relevance to the UK in particular for the three decades after 1945 and the emergence of the welfare state model. But, at the same time, the explanations derived against a US background may have been more applicable to pre-1930's Britain, and they may well be relevant again at the beginning of the 21st century, after the Thatcher-Major years and the continuity of pro-market policies under New Labour.

Under the new policy doctrine of neo-liberalism, it is argued that foundations exist to provide an alternative to some kinds of state responsibilities. The reasoning is clear: exclusively state provision of the wide range of welfare, educational, and cultural services would violate the neo-liberal ideological precept of limited government (Prewitt 1999, p. 2). In the same vein, but somewhat differently, 'For the state, foundations tend to be vehicles for semi-privatising certain tasks that are not as easily or as efficiently accomplished within the bounds of state administration' (Strachwitz quoted in Anheier and Toepler 1999b: 4).

Along similar lines, more recently it has been suggested that foundations 'reclaim societal space for a functioning civil society from what conservative observers such as Olasky (1992) regard as an overextended welfare state' (Anheier and Toepler 1999b: 5). Within a civil society context, to paraphrase Gellner (1994: 5), foundations rank among voluntary organisations and similar institutions, which, taken together, are strong enough to counterbalance the forces of the state and the market, thereby preventing the state from dominating and the market from atomising the rest of society.

The most common explanations of foundation existence and formation focus on the alleged virtues of foundations in providing sources of innovation, redistribution, policy change and challenge, an alternative to the state, providing for those 'beyond' market and state, and adopting a longer-term perspective than is possible for governments driven by electoral timetables and political expediency (see Boulding 1972; Odendahl 1990; Prewitt 1999; Anheier and Toepler 1999a; Anheier 2001).

Different types of foundations may exist as solutions to somewhat different problems. So, for example, corporate foundations may be seen as a way of defusing criticism of 'tainted money' by managing corporate donations more openly and systematically (see Burlingame 1999). Community foundations present themselves as local devices for avoiding big government, reducing the tax burden, humanising global capitalism, and crucially, maintaining, even strengthening, local control (Covington 1994; Bertelsmann Foundation 1999b).

Two important points are worth highlighting here. First, explanations of the existence of foundations are intimately intertwined with assumptions about and attitudes to the role of the state. Second, none of the explanations addresses the question why foundations exist as distinct from non-profit organisations in general: why do foundation creators not simply give their money to one or more existing charities, or indeed to public bodies? The answer may well lie less in the economics of fund distribution (see above) than in the realm of power and control over the use of assets. This is, in the first instance, achieved through the instrument of the deed, which binds assets to specified purposes and instructs trustees to act accordingly, and thereafter through trusteeship and self-perpetuating boards.

Another way of approaching the question of why foundations exist is to consider who creates them and why. Systematic data on the motivations of those creating foundations are not available for the UK. In the US the available data suggest that those with varying amounts of wealth create foundations for six main sets of reasons (Ylvisaker 1987; Odendahl 1987a, b; Ostrander and Schervish 1990; Ostrower 1995).

**Value-based motivations**

- Concern for the welfare of others, social responsibility

- Religious heritage

- Desire to repay society

- Political beliefs

- Concern with particular activities or issues

- Commitment to a specific geographical community

**Instrumental motivations**

- Flexibility of foundation as compared with other charitable options

- Tax incentives

- Establishing a vehicle for the systematic conduct of philanthropic giving

- Memorial/dynastic motives

- Family tradition of charitable activities

- Desire to create a memorial to self

- Desire to create a family institution

- Lack of heirs

**Peer pressure**

- Social pressures from peers

- Fashion

**Selfish motives**

- Maintaining some form of control over assets

- Personal satisfaction of creating a foundation.

US studies also highlight the role of particular professions such as solicitors, accountants, and financial advisers in encouraging foundation formation (Odendahl 1987a; 1990). Although we know that in the US two lawyers are concerned with a remarkably high proportion of all foundation wealth (Fitzherbert and Richards 2001: 325), there are no similar data for the UK on the role of lawyers and financial advisers in foundation creation, though several law firms in the City of London specialise in philanthropic services.

In view of the above list of motivations, it is not wholly implausible to suggest that foundations may exist as a solution to the problems of the rich rather than the poor. Foundation creators may see foundations not merely (or even primarily) as socially legitimate tax shelters, but rather as a means of: averting criticism and resentment of their wealth in a democratic society; salving their consciences (about being overly rich and about how their wealth was made or acquired) and 'paying back/making reparation'; achieving personal goals and interests; avoiding state intervention in problems in which the donor has an interest; and, crucially, doing all of this with control. Arguably, what differentiates foundation formation from other charitable giving is that in practice (though not necessarily in law) the donor and his/her family and chosen associates retain control over what is done with the gift (Odendahl 1990; Burkeman 1999; Whitaker 1974, 1979). Similar points might be made about some corporate foundations.

More recently, some foundations have been created as a 'solution' to the political and practical problems arising from the privatisation of publicly or mutually owned companies. For example, the Northern Rock Foundation derives its income from a covenant from Northern Rock plc put in place when the company moved from being mutually owned to a limited company and without which the privatisation was unlikely to have gone ahead. Although the company was created by generations of mutual owners, the (new) company now refers to its 'massive generosity' as the 'benefactor' of the foundation. In addition, a budget has been set aside from the foundation's income to be disbursed to charitable causes chosen by the chief executive of the company, and the foundation's funds are used to match the charitable giving of company staff.

## A World Without Foundations?

What would we lose if foundations were abolished? Would we reinvent them? As before, we posit claim and counterclaim.

*Claim*: *Foundations provide social benefits that outweigh their costs, and this value added would be lost if foundations were abolished or not encouraged through tax legislation.*

- *For founders*: among the forms of philanthropic activity, the foundation has proved more beneficial and reliable for donors, trustees and beneficiaries than alternative forms, in particular 'unorganised', individual philanthropy.

- *For government*: foundations are doubly useful: they add to government activities where needed and politically expedient, and they can be used as tools of government policy.

- *For civil society*: foundations are the banks of civil society; they help fund innovative, risky projects that neither market nor state would support. A functioning civil society needs independent financial institutions.

*Counterclaim*: *Foundations are an expensive way to allocate private funds for public benefit; rather than generating added value, they are a net cost to the taxpayer. Public policy should not encourage the creation of foundations, and existing foundations should be phased out.*

- *For founders*: while foundations may have been useful instruments in the past, there are now more efficient and flexible options available for philanthropic activities.

- *For government*: foundations fall into the class of tax-inefficient means of achieving public benefits; their tax-exempt status seems difficult to justify unless they meet clearly specified public needs and conform to government programmes.

- *For civil society*: foundations are cultural leftovers of the Victorian era, are continued expressions of the old class system, and are yet to become part of a modern British society that is more mobile, open, and diverse. Unless foundations modernise, they are best left where they are, namely, at the margins of modern Britain.

Why do foundations continue to exist? The simplest answer is: they exist because they are valued by society. They offer something that society would otherwise lose. Prewitt (1999) and others such as Anheier (2001) and Anheier and Toepler (1999c) suggest that the added value of foundations could take the form of voluntary redistribution of wealth, innovation, fostering change and safeguarding tradition and heritage, catering to minority demands, and advocating pluralism. Of course, empirical evidence would be needed to examine these contributions in a systematic way—evidence that we so painfully lack.

However, even if more comprehensive data were available, answers could easily be somewhat misleading. They may underestimate the institutional inertia created through the permanence of foundations in legal terms and the social and political protection they receive through the trusteeship system, with trustees typically recruited from social and professional elites. Indeed, in the case of Britain, but also for the US, one could say, with only some overstatement, that foundations are created and governed by the country's elite (Whitaker 1979). They are deeply ingrained in the country's class structure and deeply embedded in its political systems. As a result, it may in fact be more costly politically as well as economically to abolish a foundation than to allow it continue to exist, however ineffectively or obscurely.

Why we continue to allow the survival, and even encourage the further creation, of foundations in a democratic society like Britain is by no means self-evident. In the US, foundations, from their inception, have been objects of suspicion and criticism.[4] Some key themes emerge in the criticisms of foundations, including that foundations are an inappropriate use of private funds to influence public policy, that they interfere with the democratic process, and that they are founded on 'dirty money', attempting to curry public favour and rehabilitate robber-baron images, which would have been better spent on improving working conditions for their founders' employees.

---

[4] See Karl and Katz (1981); Nielsen (1972; 1979; 1985; 1996); Douglas and Wildavsky (1980–1); Odendahl (1990); Bothwell (2001). For a summary or recent criticisms, see the contributions in *Foundation News and Commentary* (May/June 1998). More recently, critiques of foundations have been published by a range of non-academic journals including *Nation, New Republic, Atlantic, Forbes, Wall Street Journal, New York Times* (early 1998 front page piece); the *Philadelphia Inquirer* (April 1993) described tax exempt foundation endowments as 'suck(ing) wealth out of the nation's tax base' (that is, foundations lock money into endowments over which they alone have control and which would otherwise have provided tax income for immediate spending on democratically decided public services). The UK voluntary sector press, (for example, *Third Sector*) focuses on service-providing charities and volunteering rather than on foundations. There is no equivalent to the *Chronicle of Philanthropy* in Britain.

In the past, the Carnegie United Kingdom Trust might have been subject to this sort of criticism. Today those foundations resulting from the privatisation of mutually owned companies, which then present themselves as great benefactors, might be similarly criticised (see the case of Northern Rock above). Somewhat differently, foundations formed from the proceeds of businesses built on arms, alcohol, tobacco, and gambling may be seen as 'tainted', but critics of such foundations sometimes fail to realise that foundations formed without such monies then go on to derive their investment income from companies with less than 'pure' records (for example, some oil or drug companies, companies with very poor industrial relations or environmental practices, especially in the Third World).

Foundations in the UK have never experienced the sort of investigation and criticism generated by the 1960's US Congressional inquiries into self-dealing, low payout rates, undue secrecy, and so on, which led to the 1969 Tax Reform Act (Peterson Commission 1970; Simon 1996; Troyer 2000). Given the traditional secrecy of UK foundations and the patchy evidence on the proportion of income paid out in grants, the absence of a systematic governmental inquiry into the practice and capacity of foundations is indeed surprising, in particular when we recall that some of the Labour governments of the 1960's and 1970s were certainty not 'foundation-friendly' and that the Conservative Thatcher-Major governments, preoccupied with efficient use of tax revenue, were in search of alternatives to public service provision. Were foundations perhaps too marginal, factually or ideologically, to warrant a closer look at their foundations by either political party?

We suggest that, for the long-term development of the British foundation sector, such reviews could have been helpful in highlighting some critical facts. Most importantly, in Britain it appears that very few foundations meet the 5 per cent payout rate that is mandatory for foundations in the US. Furthermore, some foundations in Britain find it necessary to pay significant fees to trustees for professional advice, while others have surprisingly low returns on investments, suggesting a relative loss rather than gain in funds available for public purposes. For example, in the bullish stock markets in the late 1990s, the Garfield Weston Foundation's £2.5 billion of assets could have been expected to generate an income of about £125 million a year, equivalent to the 5 per cent payout requirement in the US. In fact, however, the foundation regards £26 million as its 'normal income'—'an absurdly small amount in the circumstances' (FitzHerbert and Richards 2001: 325). But yet again more systematic research is needed to get a clearer and more systematic assessment of the financial management of UK foundation wealth.

The real answer to the question 'why UK foundations continue to exist' may lie in a mix of their invisibility, lack of political will to push alternatives, and apathy generated in part by 'foundation innocuousness', in part by their elite networks, and fuelled by the acceptance among foundation representatives about their own myths. In other words, the tendency to assume that foundations continue to exist because they have positive legitimacy, based on systematic evidence of their positive contributions to society, may be unfounded. Foundations may continue to exist simply because they are there already, very few people are aware of them or of the privileges they enjoy, they are of no real concern to politicians, are believed to do at least no more harm than good, or are otherwise seen as largely irrelevant. Getting rid of foundations would require addressing the larger and politically much more difficult problem of the definition of 'charity'. Apathy and lack of political and public interest and will may the most important factors in the continued existence of foundations.

A related explanation might be that people believe foundations' own accounts of themselves as innovators and guardians of the public good, despite the lack of systematic evidence to support those claims. Dobkin-Hall's (1996) call for US foundations to fund more dispassionate and less self-congratulatory research about the non-profit sector is equally relevant in the UK: 'Through the 1980's and mid-90's, philanthropy advocates did their best to muzzle critical research by steering money to academic centres willing to mix research and advocacy, by lavishing attention on "friendly" scholars, and by attacking independent researchers and charging that their work could lead to calls for greater government regulation' (Dobkin-Hall 1996). What British foundation, we ask following Hall, would be willing to fund critical research on philanthropy, and publicly stand by its decision to do so once the results are in and about to be published?

What would we lose if foundations were abolished? This is more than a rhetorical question. Indeed, foundations hardly exist in some countries, with France, Austria, Finland, Denmark, and Japan as prominent examples. All five countries have higher per capita incomes than the UK, rank higher on the Human Development Indicator scale (UNDP 2002), and significantly less poverty and a more equal income distribution throughout. Foundations were abolished in France following the Revolution of 1789, and have been 'reinvented' only under the somewhat restrictive umbrella of the *Fondation de France*. Nearly all Austria's foundations disappeared during the two world wars, and little attempt has been made to revive them. The Japanese government kept a close eye on foundations until the late 1990s, and foundations in Scandinavian countries are viewed with considerable suspicion (see for example, Brown, Kenny, and Turner 2000; Anheier 2001; Herberts 2001).

The standard argument that foundations lever private funds for public purposes comes in two versions. One is that foundation money would otherwise be spent or passed on to often already advantaged heirs. The other is that foundations give (small) grants that encourage others to give additional sums. These leverage arguments remain weak, however, unless two critical outcomes can be demonstrated empirically:

- the public benefits generated by foundation activities outweigh the opportunity costs of loss of tax income, that is, that potential founders would not give directly to charity assets otherwise endowed to the foundation; and

- additional monies leveraged by foundation grants actually come from private sources, including existing foundations, and not from tax revenue via public bodies.

Thus, in general and simple terms, arguments for the retention of foundations require proof that the benefits outweigh the costs. In this context, it is worth outlining the broad criticism of foundations presented by Porter and Kramer (1999: 121–30) who suggest that foundations have a responsibility to achieve a social impact disproportionate to their spending, not least because some of the money they give away belongs to the taxpayer. They reach two conclusions: too few foundations work strategically 'to do better' to achieve this disproportionate impact; and foundations are a costly way of creating social benefit.

The following example might illustrate the last point. When individuals (as opposed to foundations), contribute £100 to not-for-profit organisations, the government loses £40 in forgone tax revenue, but the recipient charity has £100 to devote to some specified public benefit. Thus, the benefit is 250 per cent of the lost tax revenue. By contrast, the case for foundations is different, and in the absence of UK figures we use US data as an illustration. On average, US foundations donate 5.5 per cent of their current asset value each a year, slightly above the prescribed payout rate of 5 per cent (see above). When $100 is contributed to a foundation, the government loses the same $40 but the immediate social benefit is only $5.50, that is, less than 14 per cent of the forgone tax revenue. At a 10 per cent discount rate the present value of the foundation's cumulative contribution after five years would be only $21, or just over 50 per cent of the lost tax revenue, and after 100 years it would be $55, or some 133 per cent of the tax lost a century earlier.

These figures demonstrate dramatically the empirical case that could be made against foundations. The example above means that taxpayers contribute up front for much of the expected social benefit that could be attributed to foundations over time. Furthermore, the delayed social benefit has to be put in the context of two additional sets of costs: administrative costs on behalf of the foundations, and costs to grantees in complying with application and reporting processes. Taking all these factors into account, Porter and Kramer (1999) conclude that foundations are a socially expensive and hence inequitable way of allocating private funds to public purposes.

For Britain, any similar calculation would also need to take into account the absence of any mandatory payout rate, and the likelihood that most foundations have payout rates well below the US average of 5.5 per cent. Moreover, these calculations would have to factor in the practice of some UK foundations of remunerating trustees, and investment incomes well below market rates of return, that are typical for many foundations, both large and small. We could make similar cases for mixed foundations, corporate foundations, and also community foundations. In each case, we argue, we would find that foundations are a costly way to achieve social benefits.

## Foundations and Democracy

What is the relationship between foundations, democracy, and civil society? Are foundations necessary for modern democratic societies to function?

*Claim*: Whatever the drawbacks of foundations, the roles they play provide benefits for society that outweigh the disadvantages associated with them.

- *For founders*: foundation offer a way for philanthropists to provide 'voice' and political space for those who would otherwise be excluded and less heard in the political process.

- *For government*: foundations open up new political options and can search for answers and approaches outside the limits of party politics; they add independent voices to the policy process.

- *For civil society*: foundations are independent bastions against the hegemony and controlling attitudes of government and big business;

they provide the pluralism needed and support the dynamic political forces of today: think tanks and NGOs.

**Counterclaim**: *There is no systematic evidence that foundations fulfil the roles claimed. Furthermore, it is doubtful whether foundations have the financial and organisational capacities to perform those roles.*

*For founders*: foundations are the province of self-righteous, self-appointed groups of do-gooders, and ultimately represent the voice of the elite and upper-middle class.

- *For government*: foundations interfere with the democratic process; they represent special interests, and rarely the public good, and should be treated as such. Foundations have no political legitimacy, nor are they democratically controlled.

- *For civil society*: foundations are undemocratic, quasi-aristocratic bastions in a modern, formally egalitarian society. For a dynamic, inclusive civil society, their elitist, fossilising, and bureaucratic characteristics make foundations more part of the problem than the solution.

The very fact that foundations can operate outside the political system of parties, government, and public administration creates opportunities for support of causes that are either bypassed or unwelcome to mainstream politics. This would include ethnic, religious, or cultural minorities, the socially excluded, or any other disadvantaged group that finds it hard to be heard by, and to get access to, political institutions. In such cases, foundations can provide support and compensate for democratic deficiencies.

The most spectacular examples are the support of the civil rights movement in the US by Ford and other foundations, and the support of the anti-Apartheid movement in South Africa by US, Dutch, and Scandinavian foundations, as well as a tiny number of UK foundations. In the UK, only 3 per cent of overall grants go specifically to ethnic minorities, but there are exceptions. Prominent examples of foundation support for minorities include the Hilden Charitable Fund, spending 33 per cent of its grant-making income on support for minorities; the Barrow Cadbury Trust and the Barrow Cadbury Fund, spending significant sums on asylum, immigration and resettlement, racial justice, disability, and gender programmes; and the Diana, Princess of Wales Memorial Fund, giving 45 per cent of all grants in 1999 to black-led charities or to projects specifically designed to meet minority ethnic requirements.

On the other side of the political spectrum, one could mention the role of conservative US foundations in sponsoring 'traditional family policies' in Congress, in promoting religious education and prayer at state schools, or in paving the way for Reagan's neo-liberal agenda in the 1980s. In the UK some foundations played a similar role in supporting Thatcher's market agenda, and in maintaining and increasing the dominance of London-based elite arts institutions.

Support for 'unpopular causes', on both sides of the political spectrum, has not gone without criticism. As noted above, one major criticism of foundations is that they are perhaps the most unaccountable organisations in democratic societies. Foundations are organisations without shareholders, voters, or customers—and their 'clients' are highly unlikely to criticise them. (Foundations seeking new donations may, however, be criticised by donors.) Foundations' lack of awareness of the need for accountability is nicely illustrated in the following quotations:

'At the foundation we—my brother and sister and I—didn't care what people thought about us, and we still don't. We simply ignore the criticism. We stopped accepting grant applications three years ago so that we can go ahead and do our own thing' (J. Roderick MacArthur Foundation: Rick MacArthur quoted in *Foundation News and Commentary*, May/June 1998). In the same vein but from a different perspective, M. Horowitz of the conservative Hudson Institute claims: 'Foundations have made a profound mistake in thinking themselves morally and intellectually superior. They're still energised by the thought of themselves holding back democratically enacted outcomes and by the idea that they're beleaguered defenders of moral virtue, standing at the gates of a good and just society' (interviewed by *Foundation Watch*, 1/2, 1997).

In the UK, although every charity is required by law to supply a copy of its most recent annual report and accounts, 15 per cent of foundations failed to do so, according to a recent survey (FitzHerbert and Richards 2001: x). Few foundations go further than the provision of what is legally required in terms of annual reports and accounts. One notable exception is Bridge House Estates Trust Fund, which holds its grants committee meetings in public, not least because its trustee is required to do so under local government openness rules.[5]

---

[5] There is, of course, an argument that public meetings would merely push the real decisions behind closed doors. But that is another debate.

There has long been debate as to whether foundations are public or private bodies (for a summary, see McIlnay 1998). One strong argument for viewing foundations as public rather than private bodies is that public accountability is built into the concept of charity via the notion of public benefit that is central to its legal definition. The tax relief and other legal privileges enjoyed by foundations are another powerful argument for viewing foundations as having a duty of public accountability. "The privacy of foundations is a privilege awarded to them because of their contributions to society, not an excuse to ignore the responsibilities of citizenship in a democracy' (McIlnay 1998: 101).

Additional arguments for accountability arise for foundations that are not fully endowed but rely on fund solicitation for some of their revenue, as is the case with community foundations. As for other fund-raising non-profit organisations, donors need to be assured that the ways in which such foundation are run and spending donated are open to public scrutiny, with easily accessible information.

A crucial argument for the accountability of foundations has to do with their roles in 'determining' public priorities in a modern democracy. The critical charge that foundations interfere with the democratic process contains three elements. First, foundations attempt directly to influence public policy (for example, via lobbying and network influence); second, foundations determine and pursue their own priorities with a mix of private and public funds (forgone tax) over which government has no control; and third, foundations fund causes and organisations which may rely on state funding in the medium to long run. The latter point is expressed in the claim that foundations are 'bribing state agencies to adopt their agendas . . . sounds innocent, but no one is fooled. The whole purpose is to lure states into expanding their bureaucracies and increasing spending, all in the name of improving public health' (McMenamin 1997).

There is little systematic data in the UK on the basis of which to assess the extent to which foundation grant-making adds to the public expenditure once foundation 'seed money' or short-term support has dried up. Several examples give the general impression that foundation funding might indeed create problems for statutory bodies left to pick up the bill for longer-term funding. One recent high-profile example was the funding of an HIV/AIDS ward at a leading London hospital that the hospital could not afford to staff and run.

The charge that foundations attempt directly to influence public policy has little force in the UK. The vast majority of foundations operates on a charitable sticking-plaster model and have remarkably little interest in policy matters. One explanation for this lack of interest may be that foundations are wary of being seen to be 'political'; another may be that they simply don't have anything to contribute beyond statements of the importance of their own existence and independence and vague platitudes about 'civil society' and the non-profit sector in general.

There are some notable exceptions, however. Foundations explicitly aspiring to influence policy include the Nuffield Foundation, the Diana Princess of Wales Memorial Fund, Joseph Rowntree Foundation, Joseph Rowntree Charitable Trust, Esmee Fairbairn Foundation, The City Parochial Foundation and the Trust for London, The Carnegie United Kingdom Trust, The Barrow Cadbury Trust and the Barrow Cadbury Fund.

These are relatively large and well-known foundations. But the criticism that foundations interfere with democratic processes assumes that foundations are actually effective in their interventions. The reality is that in the UK there are no data on the effectiveness of foundations in influencing public policy, although Joseph Rowntree Charitable Trust has recently funded research on this topic.

## The Roles of Foundations in Britain

We suggested above that one reason for the lack of public and political interest in foundations is that they could be seen as of little consequence. In terms of their financial capacity, and in comparison with both government and the voluntary sector, UK foundations operate with small change. For example, in the fields of social welfare and health (foundations' highest spending areas overall), with the exception of medical research, government outspends foundations by about 100 to one (Trust and Foundation News, December 2001: 36). Yet, despite their modest resources, foundations have presented themselves as playing vital roles in society.

What are these vital roles and what evidence is there to suggest that foundations fulfil the expectations they entail? We will take a brief look

at several of the roles that have been suggested in the literature (see Prewitt, 1999; Anheier and Toepler 1999c; Anheier 2001).

### The role of foundations is to redistribute resources from rich to poor

The idea that the major role of foundations is to engage in and promote redistribution of resources fits with the popular and historical image of helping the poor and needy. This role also fits with many, especially 19th-century, philanthropists' descriptions of their motives for giving in terms of giving back, paying dues, and perhaps betrays moral uneasiness about the size of the divide between rich and poor.

Certainly, today many foundations deliberately adopt a policy of funding work in especially disadvantaged communities hoping in some way to equalise the distribution of resources. Redistribution of resources is obviously an attractive goal, for several reasons. One is that it helps to create a fairer society without radical, social, and economic upheaval. Another is that it is essential to the longer-term sustainability of existing social and economic arrangements. In other words, redistribution is a way of dealing with the damaging side effects of a market system.

But there are various problems with redistribution as a primary or sole justification for the existence of foundations. Perhaps the two most important weaknesses in this approach are that:

- It is not clear that foundation giving overall actually is redistributive. Indeed, a large proportion of total foundation giving undoubtedly goes to support areas of interest and geographical areas that are very far from the needs and interests of most disadvantaged groups in society. For example, only 3 per cent of foundation funding overall goes to support ethnic minority issues; considerable funding goes to the opera, ballet, and other elite interests, primarily in London. The 'London bias' is repeated in overall giving. Whereas grants in London provide £35 per head of population, less than £5 per head of population is given in Northern Ireland, West Midlands, Wales,

Yorkshire and Humber, and North-East regions (FitzHerbert and Richards 2001: v; see also Vincent and Pharoah, 2000).[6]

- Even if foundations did actually spend the bulk of their money in redistributive ways, it is not clear that the outcome would be as redistributive as, or any more redistributive than, it would have been had foundation funds been taxed and spent by the state (Prewitt 1999). In other words, foundations would have to be highly redistributive relative to forgone tax revenue.

**The role of foundations is to promote innovation**

Promoting innovation in social perceptions, values, relationships, and ways of doing things has long been a role ascribed to foundations. Innovation is a goal pursued by foundations working in a wide range of areas in science, research, the arts, health, social welfare, and the environment.   The role of promoting innovation is attractive to foundations for several reasons. One is that it provides an apparently simple demarcation line between the role of government and that of foundations. Another is that, in the past, it has served as a way of restricting foundation involvement to manageable proportions. If foundations exist to support innovation, this enables them legitimately to engage in short-term funding. Once something is no longer innovative foundations may pull out with a clear conscience and move on to another piece of short-term support. The foundation has done its job. Picking up the ongoing longer-term bill is someone else's concern.

---

[6] These figures may reflect the way in which data are collected, again underlining the need for more and better research.

Another reason why supporting innovation is said to be especially suited to foundations is that their lack of accountability to constituents and customers means that they can run ahead of public opinion. They can take the risk of buying art or putting on performances the public may not initially like, they can fund research and experiments that may turn out to be a dead end, they can support work with drug users, paedophiles, asylum seekers, and other groups commanding less than total public sympathy. This ability to take risks has led recently to a currently fashionable view of foundations as social venture capitalists. This view has subsequently been developed by various writers and has also been challenged as a dangerous model encouraging over-involvement, even interference, by grant-makers (see, for example, Letts, Ryan, and Grossman 1997; Sievers 1997).[7]


But whether foundations succeed in promoting innovation is open to question. First, because foundations are reluctant to spend money building up and maintaining a sound knowledge base, it is not clear that foundations are actually capable of distinguishing truly innovative work from what is merely new or even 'repackaged' work. The failure of foundations to spend money on dissemination, and if necessary replication, means that money spent on innovation is sometimes just an expensive candle snuffed out too quickly. There is nothing efficient or socially effective about funding innovation unless processes are in place to learn and communicate positive and negative lessons to the wider society. Innovations are ultimately sustainable and valuable only if resources are available for development and maintenance, as we will discuss below. Foundations generally do not see this as their

---

[7] We new models of philanthropy in more detail in Chapters 4 and 5.

responsibility and governments are increasingly unwilling to take on the funding of innovations initiated by foundations.

## The role of foundations is to promote social change

Closely related to innovation is the role of creating or promoting social change that is frequently ascribed to foundations, not least by foundations themselves (Prewitt 1999). Several somewhat different versions of the social change role are ascribed to foundations. These include:

- promoting radical structural change (most commonly attributed to some US foundations at certain periods in history by their conservative critics);

- fostering recognition of new needs and 'giving voice';

- 'oak trees from acorns' that is, funding small-scale, often local, projects from which it is hoped that larger, wider-scale activities will grow;

- changing the way in which we think about social issues and their solutions and adding to the cultural and political menu;

- increasing participation and empowerment of people excluded from policy and practice solutions;

- demonstrating the feasibility of new ways of working; and

- encouraging exploration of new ideas and cultural forms.

The notion that foundations can or do promote social change has always had its critics. As one leading American practitioner and commentator wrote at the time of the congressional inquiry into US foundations:

"The great myth about foundations today is that they are firmly ensconced on the leading edge of social change, managed by far sighted trustees and staff who make brilliantly daring decisions about the disposition of the funds over which they have stewardship. In this myth the funds are known as seed corn and venture capital thereby associating the foundation vicariously with two of the noblest traditions in American life, the agrarian and the entrepreneurial. But foundations in fact have a highly restricted capacity to influence social change. This is so because in most cases the funds at their disposal are too small to have sufficient leverage and because the very nature of fiduciary management and spending of trust funds makes for caution. Furthermore, foundations may sense that the public is uneasy about having them play too influential a role in determining where the society is headed, and this awareness is inhibiting to them" (Pifer 1968:11).

Curiously, examples of foundations creating major social change, despite in some cases huge aggregate expenditure over many years, are hard to find. For example, despite the hundreds of thousands of pounds spent in recent years on racial justice by (mostly Quaker) foundations, this had failed to touch the institutional racism revealed by the Stephen Lawrence Inquiry. Similarly, despite the many beneficial effects of the Carnegie United Kingdom Trust's 'Third Age Programme', the Trust itself notes its failure to have discrimination against people on the basis of their age made unlawful. Clearly positive examples are Cadbury's funding of the Runnymede Trust, the Joseph Rowntree Charitable Trust's contribution to the signing of the Amsterdam Treaty, and, much further back, Carnegie's support for public libraries. Of course, one has to acknowledge the difficulty of pointing to the precise contributions foundations made to social change, and a greater research effort is clearly called for to examine the issue more fully. At the same time, a few swallows do not make a summer. Had foundations roles been more than marginal in bringing about social change, specific examples would be easier to identify, the rule rather than the exception.

## The role of foundations is to preserve traditions and cultures

At the same time, some foundations specifically play the role of preserving traditions, ideas, cultural artefacts (for example, the National Trust) and, more generally, the existing social order (see, for example, Fischer 1983). The social change and preserving tradition approaches to the role of foundations is obviously subject to the criticism above that in real life David rarely beats Goliath. Both roles—promoting change and preserving tradition—require recognition of three important factors.

First, the more effective foundations are in achieving or opposing change, the more likely they are to encounter strong public opposition from interests not served by those changes. Second, there is a view that foundations cannot operate on a scale that is transformative if they work alone. Without assistance from government and the market, foundation interventions are likely to be swamped by larger social, cultural, and economic forces. Third, how powerful foundations can be in promoting or resisting social change depends in part on the theory of social change in which one believes: do ideas 'drive' history, or are technological development, the power of social movements, market incentives, government interventions, or indeed moral exhortation the key factors (see Prewitt 1999)?

## The role of foundations is to promote pluralism

Promoting pluralism is the role many foundations ascribe to themselves, particularly in the US, and some commentators like Prewitt (1999) see the promotion of pluralism as the most persuasive argument for the existence and legitimacy of foundations.[8] The promoting pluralism role takes various forms:

- promoting social experimentation and diversity in general;

- curbing the dominance of government in modern society (see Karl and Katz 1981), and serving as antidote to state control of social, economic, cultural, and environmental policy (see, for example, Alchon1985); and

- protecting dissent and civil liberties (Ostrander 1993; 1994; McIlnay 1998; Dowie 2001).

For example, Prewitt, in a speech at 2nd International Foundation Symposium in Germany, suggested that foundations could fund the unusual or the unexpected because

"they are not beholden to the consensus forcing demands placed on the public sector. In short, foundations can intensify the natural diversity of the non-profit sector, and thereby contribute to pluralism. Here, then, is a justification for the foundation sector. Not redistribution, not efficiency, not even social change though some amount of all those occur but an ongoing and lasting contribution to the pluralism of practice and thought and via that contribution a deep commitment to the principles of tolerance and openness that flow from pluralism" (Prewitt 1999).

---

[8] It should be noted that the pluralism argument, which finds it clearest expression in the writings on Prewitt, has a long history in policy debates about the role of foundations, most prominently in the US Senate Report on Finance (1965) in the run-up to the 1968-9 reforms: 'private philanthropic organisations can be uniquely qualified to initiate thought and action, experiment with new and untried ventures, dissent from prevailing attitudes, and act quickly and flexibly. Equally important, because their funds are frequently free of commitment to specific operating programs, they can shift the focus of their interest and their financial support from one charitable area to another. They can, hence, constitute a powerful instrument for evolution, growth, and improvement' (cited in Ridings 1999: 45).

Note that this requires an acceptance of lack of 'consensus forcing demands', and the assumptions that foundations are pluralist in their funding (which evidence suggests they are not; see Vincent and Pharoah 2000) and that those they fund are 'pluralist' (and, of course, that pluralism per se, rather than pluralism which promotes the ends of which the speaker approves, is desirable).

**The role of foundations is to promote policy and practice change**

This approach to the key role of foundations obviously has close relationships to some of those already outlined above. It is worth distinguishing, however, because some see it as a more focused and realistic role for foundations than those outlined above, which are both more ambitious in their aspiration and more difficult to assess. Again, there are different versions or elements in this role:

- examining public policy (see, for example, Reeves 1969);

- shaping public opinion (see, for example, Arnove 1980; Roelofs 1984/5);

- developing social and other research regarding social ills and government policy (see, for example, Bulmer 1999);

- coping with government failure and adopting a longer view beyond the time frame of electoral timetables;

- promoting integrated planning and service provision related to real people;

- experiences and problems in overcoming departmental and professional divisions;

- providing a space for discussion and expression of values which fit neither government nor market logic (see, for example, Nielsen 1985).

US studies of foundation roles, especially in health care reform, have shown how effective they may be in providing a basis for policy discussion. Foundations were viewed as credible actors, non-partisan in their approaches, and concerned with the public interest. They also got good marks for adequate levels of investment and timeliness of intervention in the policy process (Abramson and Spann 1998). But US foundations frequently failed fully to exploit these opportunities and policy-makers viewed foundation timidity and lack of adequate communications strategies and products as major constraints on their effectiveness in the policy arena (Abramson and Spann 1998: 10). Unfortunately, there are no similar data on policy-makers' attitudes to foundation contributions in the UK.

Foundations' potential in influencing public policy is demonstrated by the effects of the systematic communications strategy adopted by conservative foundations in the US. The policy messages funded by these foundations—chiefly deregulation, privatisation, and massive reductions in government spending—have been so aggressively marketed that they have transformed the parameters of national policy debate (Covington 1997). These foundations gave money to think tanks and others, with the general focus of the grants being to multiply the number of institutional voices conveying the same core policy agenda. In other fields, few foundations have adopted similar concerted marketing and communication strategies and few have been so successful in influencing policy agendas.

How much of the above is rhetoric and wishful thinking? Do British trusts and foundations really contribute that much to society? At present, we do not know what roles foundations adopt and in what combinations. Do foundations even have a view of their roles? Are they more likely to behave as givers distributing their largesse in small presents to good causes, rather than investing or collaborating in strategically chosen enterprises (Leat 1992)?

## Foundations as Idea and Model

In this chapter we have discussed some of the key issues relating to foundations' existence and roles in a democracy. These issues set the scene for the more detailed discussion of the future of foundations in Britain in the following chapters. The roles set out above are ones that foundations claim for themselves or have had ascribed to them. Olasky (1992), in examining what foundations actually do against what they say they intend to do, reaches a sombre conclusion in a book aptly entitled *The Tragedy of American Compassion*. We cannot say to what extent Olasky's indictment applies to the UK, as there is very little systematic data on what UK foundations actually do, and the very sparse evidence available suggests that foundations may well fall some way short of the claims above (Vincent and Pharoah 2000; Fitzherbert and Richards 2001).

Against this disappointing record, however incomplete, is there any reason to suppose that foundations could play the roles outlined above? We have already suggested that foundations in the UK have very limited financial capacity to engage in these roles in a significant way. But would they have the organisational capacity to bear the critical policy roles ascribed to them?

Some criticisms of US foundations seem equally likely to apply to UK foundations. For Covington (1997), the thinking in foundations appears small, non-strategic, and non-visionary, and Schumann (1998) concludes that the basic problem is that too much money is spent 'foolishly'. McIlnay (1998: 11) argues that foundations follow rather than start things. For example, the civil rights movement began in 1955 with the Montgomery bus boycott, but foundation grants were not significant until 1962. 'Foundation grants to organisations directly serving women and minorities have been minuscule, dispelling the myth that foundations are crusaders for social change and contradicting the descriptions that foundations have given of themselves'. Odendahl (1990: 27) reaches a rather negative conclusion about the role of foundations in US society. She charges that: 'The rich do not give to the poor but to institutions they use and cherish—the charity of the wealthy doesn't just begin at home, it stays there'. It seems that foundations build cuckoo clocks and pass them off as cathedrals; from a social change perspective, it seems that foundations do not question or probe the system: they are the system.

Why does an institution that, at least on face value, appears inherently good and beneficial fall so far short of its intentions? One major reason may be the way in which foundations typically operate, in particular their grant-making principles, selection processes, organisational cultures, staffing and trustee system. Perhaps the basic idea of a foundation is sound and desirable, but the practical model is problematic and fraught with difficulties. We consider these and related issues, focusing on the capacity of foundations for innovation and renewal, in the following chapter.

# Chapter 3

# Foundations:
# Innovation and Renewal

*Never has so much money led to so few changes.* (Ralph Nader)

*The profile of their activities is largely conventional, not reformist. They are overwhelmingly institutions of social continuity not change'* (Nielsen 1972)

*The heroic role that these trusts have allegedly played has been largely a self-generated legend. With some remarkable exceptions, older foundations became, and have for too long remained, drag anchors on American social, political, and scientific programs, choosing, it seems, to slow forward motion in order to avoid some perceived obstacle.* (Dowie 2001)

*Foundations embody an opportunity for social progress. Foundations must show that they are pioneers, capable of identifying new approaches.* (Reinhard Mohn, founder of the Bertelsmann Foundation, 1999a: 12)

*Through their willingness to innovate and take risks, foundations make significant contributions to social and sustainable development.* (C. Koch-Weser, former Managing Director of the World Bank Group, 1999: 32)

*In the midst of our work, we must not forget to capitalize on the fact that we are instruments of the extraordinary human impulse to make society a better place for all people. If not foundations, then who? It is at the very core of our being.* (Dorothy S. Ridings, President and CEO, Council of Foundations, Washington, DC: 1999: 46)

# Introduction

As we saw in Chapter 2, the *raison d'être* of foundations rests on their contribution to pluralism—or in our words: their innovative pursuit of pluralism. Prewitt (1999: 29) argues that: 'If foundations can help create and preserve pluralism, can help in the search for common human values without losing sight of the diversity of belief and practice, they will have a legitimate place in our open society'. This proposition is, as we have argued, ultimately a weak statement in support of the significant privileges foundations enjoy, in particular their favourable tax treatment and the right to operate with a minimum of public oversight and accountability.

For us, the case for foundations could be significantly strengthened if the privileges they enjoyed demonstrably made possible the *innovative pursuit* of pluralism. In other words, by having their assets and incomes exempt from taxation, and by enjoying a quasi-aristocratic position seemingly unaffected by modern institutional governance, foundations become the source of social innovation. By doing so, foundations add to the problem-solving capacity of modern societies. For example, foundations seek out fields—old, new or emerging—and identify issues and needs for support in innovative ways and means. Thus, the signature characteristic of foundations, namely, their specific capacity to innovate, is based on their freedom from the constraints of both the market and the state. Accordingly, the lack of democratic accountability is a virtue and the source of their freedom to innovate, or to support innovation, for the common good.

Do foundations in this country and the UK more broadly live up to the claims regarding innovation and pluralism? If they do not currently do so, why is this the case, and, importantly, under what conditions would they have the capacity to become more innovative? More fundamentally, how do and could foundations 'renew' themselves to remain relevant to contemporary notions of public benefit and pluralism?

## Distinctions

We will initially explore these questions in two related but distinct aspects of foundation activities:

- *setting of priorities*:  selecting the fields and areas foundations work in, and the specific needs they address; and

- *processes*:  the ways and means by which identified needs are met and programmes developed and implemented in the fields selected as priorities, including grantee selection, types of resource transfer, relationships with grantees, monitoring and evaluation.

### Table 2: Innovation and Foundations

| INNOVATIVE GRANT-MAKING | INNOVATIVE FIELD SELECTION / NEEDS IDENTIFICATION | |
|---|---|---|
| | NO | YES |
| NO | Conventional funding body | Needs/field-oriented innovator |
| YES | Ways and means-oriented innovator | Philanthropic innovator |

These distinctions are important for two reasons. First, foundations may be 'conservative' in their priorities and/or the organisations they fund, but innovative in the types of work funded. Moreover, foundation may be innovative in the priorities they set but conventional in the way they select grantees and the types of grants they make. Table 2 shows some ideal-type combinations among the two principal aspects or dimensions of innovations:

- Some foundation are conventional in the sense that they support activities in fields that are well understood and highly 'organised' in terms of other institutions involved (government and so on), where the needs are known and predictable, as are the funding mechanisms and grant recipients. For example, the Viscount Amory's Charitable Trust spends the majority of its (small) income on grants to various schools, the National Trust, Scouts, the County Agricultural Association, and sailing for young people. But 'traditionalism' is not confined to smaller foundations. The Bernard Sunley Charitable Foundation with an income approaching £3 million a year would also come into this category (see below).

- By contrast, other foundations seek out new fields and ways of funding that may go beyond what might be regarded as conventional approaches in grantee relations or funding strategies. These are what we label the philanthropic innovators. Examples in this category include some aspects of the Barrow Cadbury Trust, Charity Know How, and Esmee Fairbairn Foundation (see below).

- In between are mixed types. On the one hand, there are foundations that work in conventional fields but use innovative ways and means of putting their funds to better use; on the other hand are foundations that use conventional approaches for funding programmes on innovative topics, new needs, or emerging issues.

For example, the Architectural Heritage Trust works in a conventional field but uses a mix of grants and interest-free loans. The Wates Foundation works in fairly conventional ways to support some unusual causes; in recent years, it has given grants for work with people with learning disabilities who have been sexually abused or are in danger of committing such abuse, and for work with families of people who have committed seriously violent crimes.

In this chapter, we explore the proposition that the basic dilemma for foundations is that over time their organisational form makes them more likely to become conventional funding bodies than the innovative institutions serving the public good stipulated by Prewitt and others. By implication, if this proposition were proved correct, the policy challenge would be to find ways and means by which foundations could renew their innovative capacity, and thereby remain true to the rationale of the privileges they enjoy. Thus, the legitimacy of foundations ultimately rests on their ability to stay away from becoming instruments for the disbursement of conventional funding. Society, as we will argue below, has mechanisms more suitable for conventional funding purposes than foundations. Equitable and effective taxation and a well-functioning system of public administration are two cases in point.

Certainly, not all foundations have become, let alone remain, philanthropic innovators; yet if the claim that they contribute to pluralism and innovations is to hold true, they must be more than simple distributors of funds for specified causes and recipients. To meet the challenge Prewitt (1999) and others posit, foundations must be more than private and tax-sheltered mechanisms for distributing funds for worthy causes; indeed, either the purpose or the approach taken must involve some added value that justifies the privileges afforded to foundations.   That added value is innovation, and specifically the innovative support of initiatives that serve the common good and contribute to pluralism.

Of course, 'innovation' itself is a complex idea, and its meaning is not always clear, both generally and in specific circumstances.  By innovation we understand a special kind of change that rests on a new idea applied to initiating or improving an activity, service, or product. 'Innovation is the generation, acceptance, and implementation of new ideas, processes, products or services' (Kanter 1983:20). Innovations can involve radical breakthroughs, significant procedural modifications, or minor improvement or 'architectural' changes.  For example, the development and marketing of small personal computers has transformed the home as well as the way we work.

Not all innovations are basically technical in nature, and some are primarily about new ways of 'seeing' issues, conceptualising phenomena, and 'framing' problems.   These paradigmatic shifts may occur less frequently than procedural and programmatic innovations, but they tend to lead to some of the most profound changes. For example, the realisation in the 19th century that many diseases were spread by poor living conditions led to the rise of public health programmes.

Kanter (1983) suggests that successful innovations typically display a distinctive combination of characteristics. First, innovation involves a significant degree of uncertainty in the sense that process and outcome may be difficult to predict. Second, innovations are *knowledge-intensive* as those close to the locus of innovation tend to possess most knowledge about the definition of the situation, the process involved, and the possible outcomes, at least at the initial stage. Third, innovations are typically *controversial* as they tend to confront established interests and may take resources away from alternative uses. Fourth, and finally, innovations tend to *reach across established boundaries* in organisations, fields, or sectors.

To say that innovations involve a willingness to act under uncertainty, that they require knowledge as well as a commitment to anticipate and deal with controversies, and that they demand an ability to look across 'borders' does not mean that all four characteristics have to be present for innovative activities to take place. However, such innovations are more likely to remain unsuccessful and may fail to persuade stakeholders and other interested parties to adopt the change. For example, foundations could make decisions under uncertainty and on the basis of a good understanding of the issues, yet ultimately shy away from controversy. Others may be ready to develop controversial programmes but fail to learn from lessons in neighbouring fields, for example among other non-profit organisations or public agencies.

In most cases, however, few 'pure' innovations occur, and it is frequently the importation and modification of ideas from different circumstances, or the pursuit of analogous problem-solving techniques from quite different fields and contexts, that lead to innovative approaches. For example, venture philanthropy imports the idea and analogous investment approach from the field of finance into the field of philanthropy; similarly, the routine processing of large numbers of grant applications according to set and standardised assessment criteria reflects the procurement process of government contracting.

Behind this reasoning is an insight of organisational theory, which sees innovations as closely connected to two basic processes that drive organisational change: recombination and refunctionality (Romanelli 1991; Aldrich 1999). Recombination involves the introduction of new elements into an existing organisation, for example benchmarking and other corporate management tools in grant evaluation, or corporate responsibility programmes in businesses.  Refunctionality means the relocation of one form in a different context, for example,  the migration of for-profit financial institutions into fields previously populated primarily by foundations.

Both processes imply that what is, or has been, the field of foundation activities and expertise cannot be taken for granted and is subject to change.  In the introductory passages of this chapter we suggested that the world around philanthropy has changed significantly, while philanthropy itself has changed much less.  The signature element of foundations, namely,  the innovative pursuit of social goals, requires change in terms of recombinations and refunctionality to maintain and strengthen the distinctive features of philanthropy.  In other words, to be and remain innovative over time, foundations have to be outward-looking organisations (recombination), and somewhat 'footloose' and migrate to new fields and topics if their competitive advantage is surpassed by that of other institutions such as business, non-profit service providers, or government agencies.

Yet the very form of foundations makes it difficult for such processes of change and renewal to develop. The extent to which the organisational form of foundations makes it in fact difficult to remain innovative cannot, therefore, be underestimated. It is easier for foundations to become conventional funding bodies set in their ways than to remain flexible, change-oriented, and innovative. In so far as foundations are subject to pressures for renewal they tend to become niche funders, addressing particular problems for specific clientele adopting predictable, stable patterns of disbursement or following the fashion of the moment.

Against the context of organisational theory, we can identify some of the key challenges foundations face in fulfilling their *raison d'être*, that is, innovative contributions to public benefit. The first one is the tension between the will of the donor, as specified in the original deed, and the need for change, to adjust the vision and operation of the foundation to changing circumstances. Clearly, the more precise the stipulations of the deed and the more finely specified objectives, modes of operations, and recipients are, the more difficult innovations are likely to become over time. Conversely, a deed that leaves the mission and objectives of a foundation wide open and with little guidance can easily lead to a highly politicised and 'lost' institutions over time. Yet it remains an open question whether the primacy of the deed does prevent foundations from *remaining* innovative and flexible over time. As we will argue in Chapter 5, foundations require 'creative deeds' to allow for both change and continuity. Second, in most organisations it is outside economic or political pressures that act as the driving forces behind innovations. Yet foundations are largely shielded from such corrective and creative influences. They have no owners or electorates with clear incentives to monitor performance or, more fundamentally, the fit between mission and programme activities. As a result, the innovative character of a foundation will largely depend of the board or trustees. The board, however, is bound by the deed and the rules and regulations of the Charity Commission (see below), and cannot act with the same flexibility and managerial repertoire as corporate boards. In fact, foundation boards have typically much less flexibility than the trustees of other non-profit organisations.

Third, it becomes clear that, for foundations, the most critical decision about innovation is likely to be taken at the time when the original deed is being discussed and 'set in stone'. At present, we do not have systematic knowledge of the extent to which deeds are flexible and contain room for innovations to take place. Deeds can be restricted in a variety of ways. Some foundations are geographically restricted; for example, the Cripplegate Foundation, established in 1891, was until recently restricted to the ancient Parish of St Giles Without, Cripplegate and St Luke's Old Street, and estimated that its income represented £90–£100 per head of the population.

Some foundations are, or were, restricted in purpose; for example, a foundation in South Wales whose sole purpose was to purchase mop caps for virgins living in a particular area of Cardiff (Chesterman 1979). Other foundations have restricted purposes but considerable freedom of interpretation. The various foundations created by Joseph Rowntree are good examples here. The foundations are restricted to addressing the causes of social problems but Joseph Rowntree had the foresight explicitly to give his future trustees the freedom to interpret this in ways relevant to contemporary perceptions.

The very decision to establish a foundation as charitable can be highly restrictive, as the Aberfan Disaster Fund illustrates. In this case the Fund trustees found themselves constantly at odds with the Charity Commission in spending the money in the ways in which the trustees and the families of Aberfan wanted (McLean and Johnes 2000). Similar problems arose in relation to Band Aid, and more recently, in allocating the funds raised after 11 September 2001, where funds were created as charitable organisations.

Finally, it is important to distinguish between innovation and renewal of individual foundations and that of the foundation sector as a whole. There may be an implicit division of labour or interaction between conventional and innovative foundations, which produces an overall greater impact. For example, with some foundations engaged in 'standard' funding of 'conventional' social service delivery organisations, others can target new needs and experiment with new ideas and approaches. In other words, while older foundations may become more conservative and conventional funders over time, the sector as a whole may be more innovative through the entry of new foundations with new purposes and priorities and different styles of grant-making.

## Innovative Grant-Making?

One example of a traditionalist funder is the Bernard Sunley Charitable Foundation. This foundation prides itself on being 'policy free', despite the fact that it clearly makes choices between grant applicants: 'Regarding our policy . . . our objectives are wide open to any charity anywhere in the world. I would have thought that nothing could be clearer than that' (quoted in FitzHerbert, Forrester, and Grau 1997:

251). The list of grantees and the size of grants appear to vary little from year to year. Typical beneficiaries are 'the older universities and cathedrals, uniformed youth groups, national associations and major fundraising charities' (FitzHerbert, Forrester, and Grau 1997: 253).

Geographical grant distribution bears little relation to the distribution or severity of needs addressed. In 1995–6 no grants were made in Northern Ireland, Wales received £0.52 per 1,000 population, whereas the south of England received £46.97 per 1,000 population. This distribution may simply reflect the number and quality of applications from each area. 'Where individual trustees have made the foundation relatively well known in the vicinity of their country homes, thus generating a disproportionate number of applications from these areas, the foundation has said that it is happy for this to be reflected in the grants it makes' (FitzHerbert, Forrester, and Grau 1997: 252).

The Bernard Sunley Charitable Foundation highlights some interesting issues and tensions around the notion of 'foundations as innovators'. For many charities the very stability of the foundation's list of grant recipients and size of grants must be welcomed as an antidote to the practices of those foundations which pick up and drop projects from year to year in their constant search for 'innovation'. Without a coherent and adequate vision and mission providing the basis for the foundation, there is a danger that 'innovation' can become indistinguishable from irresponsible promiscuity, whereby foundations father numerous dependent offspring only to move on to the next new and exciting affair.

As noted above, some foundations are innovative in their choice of priorities and approaches to support. For example, as early as 1995 the priorities of the Barrow Cadbury Trust included 'the settlement needs of refugees where initiatives can effect changes in policy and practice; and the rights of asylum seekers, refugees and immigrants'. Before venture philanthropy became prominent among funders, the Barrow Cadbury Trust stressed its desire to work as a partner with those it funds and the responsibilities of trustees in assessing and visiting projects.

Charity Know How (now Allavida) is another example of an innovative grant-maker. Charity Know How was established in 1991 by a group of existing foundations and the Foreign Office to support the emergence of the third sector in central and eastern Europe and the republics of the former Soviet Union by making grants for skill-sharing partnerships. Esmee Fairbairn Foundation's recently announced Rethinking Crime and Punishment programme combines grant-making, research, evaluation, and dissemination, coordinated by a director and a specially created Supervisory Board. The Supervisory Board comprises Trustees, members of the judiciary, academics, and people from business and the media. The overall aim of this £3 million project is to raise the level of public debate about how to deal with offenders.

Examples of other traditionalist and innovative foundations could be included here. At present there are no systematic data on how foundations fall into conventional or innovative clusters in terms of priorities and programmes. Again, there is a huge gap in our knowledge of what foundations actually do and why. The impression we gained from the available evidence, however, is that innovative foundations are the exceptions.

Vincent and Pharoah (2000) carried out a pioneering study of foundation grant-making in the UK. The evidence they were able to examine suggests that foundations are not particularly innovative in their choice of priorities. The majority of grants by number and total value go to social care, followed by health and education. Religious activities attract a substantial minority of grants, and the rest are spread thinly over wide range of areas. Science and technology attract the lowest number of grants but highest mean grant size (Table 3).

The dominance of social care grants is redolent of 19th century charity and, perhaps, an overly conservative view of the needs of disadvantaged people. As Vincent and Pharoah (2000: 29) note: 'the needs of specific beneficiary groups are perceived principally in terms of social care. There is less attention to other difficulties that might be experienced such as access to education, employment, sustainable environments and so on.'

### Table 3: Estimates for Total Grant Expenditure in Main Subject Areas

| Field | £ million | % of total grants expenditure |
|---|---|---|
| Social care | 233 | 25 |
| Health | 174 | 19 |
| Education | 155 | 17 |
| Arts/culture/recreation | 95 | 10 |
| Religious activities | 76 | 8 |
| Development/housing | 42 | 5 |
| Environment/animals | 30 | 3 |
| Philanthropy/volunteering | 30 | 3 |
| Science and technology | 24 | 3 |
| Civil society/law/advocacy | 23 | 3 |
| International | 20 | 2 |
| Social science | 14 | 2 |
| **Sub-total classified** | **916** | **100** |
| Uncoded to main subject | 64 | |
| Total grant-making | 980 | |

*Source*: Vincent and Pharoah (2000: 25).

There are several critical patterns in the distribution of grant-making that suggest that British foundations do not, on the surface at least, take approaches that respond to the nature of social problems in this country.

- Three-quarters of religious grants go to Christian causes, and 24 per cent to Jewish causes. Muslims are specifically mentioned in only 1 per cent of grants examined by Vincent and Pharoah (2000).

- Three per cent of all grants specifically mention black and ethnic minority needs (it is, of course, possible that other grants addressed these needs).

- Seven per cent of grants are for international causes, but at only £20 million in total this category is next to lowest in value.

With some exceptions, foundations do not appear to inhabit the multi-ethnic, multi-faith, and increasingly cosmopolitan society that is characteristic of modern Britain. It is, however, worth noting here that there are some, but perhaps significant, differences between smaller and larger foundations in patterns of grant-making. For example, small trusts give their largest grants in the categories of civil society, law, and advocacy.

Several other points are worth noting from Vincent and Pharoah's (2000: 64, 72, 73) survey:

- Grant size is related to general principles within trusts, and not just the needs of the project or proposal; in other words, foundations, not needs, determine expenditures.

- Grant-makers as a whole tend to approach problems similarly, which suggest a considerable degree of conformity in the way foundations address needs.

- At the same time, grant-making reveals strong patterns of 'fashion' across foundations.

- Local trusts tend to share the same main priorities as local authorities, which indicates that foundations frequently either are substitutes for council responsibilities or provide leverage to public funding.

- There are significant gaps between grant-makers' stated preferences and their overall patterns of giving. For example, some foundations express preferences for funding housing and

  accommodation, elderly people, and the environment but in reality spend very little in these categories.

Again, these points do little to support the argument that foundations are a significant force for social change. The evidence suggests that the public images foundations present when it comes to their stated grant-making preferences are somewhat more 'radical' than actual patterns of funding. Once again, the discrepancy may be a function of inadequacies in data collection and analysis. But foundations need to play their part by providing records that properly reflect what they do.

However, the fact that the broad priorities of foundations do not appear to be addressing new issues, less popular causes, and less mainstream needs does not necessarily imply that they have no innovative capacity. Thus it is important to refine our original question and ask: what are the sources of innovation and renewal in the foundation sector? What are the sources of innovation and renewal within individual foundations? It may be, of course, that innovation and renewal within the wider sector actually prompts innovation and renewal within both established and newly created foundations.

# Sources of Innovation and Renewal in Foundations

Questions about innovation and renewal in foundations raise more fundamental questions about sources of change in organisations generally, how knowledge moves between and within organisations, the roles of change agents, and who they are. Very broadly there are three approaches to explaining change in organisations:

- the *natural selection model* emphasising external determination of the fate of the organisation (Aldrich 1999);

- *resource dependency theories* emphasising the way in which organisations change as they negotiate resources (Gronbjerg 1998); and

- *institutional theory* which suggests that organisations seek legitimacy in a social context and change in order to fit prevailing norms and expectations (Powell and DiMaggio 1991).

What is interesting about the first two theories is how little relevance they appear to have to endowed foundations, at least at first sight: endowed foundations are in major respects self-sufficient organisations and not, in any obvious sense, beholden to or dependent on external forces. For the same reason it is debatable whether institutional theory applies to foundations.  Yet, as we argued, foundations like all institutions seek and require legitimacy and reputation.

A somewhat different approach to organisational change sees three clusters of forces creating motion in and around organisations: relations between organisations and their environments, growth through the life cycle, and the constant struggle for power between stakeholders within the organisation (Kanter, Stein, and Jick 1992). In other words, change within organisations is a product of external and internal factors that are related to the organisational life cycle and mediated through power relations within the organisation, in particular its form of governance. Thus, questions regarding sources of innovation and renewal within foundations are intimately bound up with the locus and distribution of power: the trustees.

**Trustees**

In theory and in law, trustees are the major source of power in foundations. They have the right and the responsibility to determine the direction of the foundation within the constraints of the trust deed that usually allows for some amount of reinterpretation in the light of changing circumstances (see below on the constraints of the trust deed). Trustees are guardians of the mission of the foundation and are legally responsible for the direction of the foundation and everything done in its name. In theory too, trustees and non-executive board members act as 'boundary spanners' (Middleton 1987); half in and half out of the organisation, they interpret the environment to the foundation and the foundation to the environment.

In reality, however, the ability of trustees to influence change within the foundation is likely to vary, partly in relation to both the type of foundation and its stage in the life cycle. A living donor is likely to effectively reduce the power of trustees. Even after death, the donor's influence may remain strong if trustees feel an obligation to do 'what the donor would have wanted'. Whatever the merits of this approach, continuing to do what a donor 'would have wanted' 20 or more years previously is unlikely to be a recipe for change.

Dowie (2001) uses the example of family foundations to suggest four stages of foundation development. In the first phase, the donor and his or her family control the foundation. In the second phase, control of the foundation passes to trustees connected to the founder or the family. 'At this point in their development, many foundations are paralysed by disagreements among trustees (regarding strategies and priorities) and remain so for months, sometimes years; in the worst cases, they are unable to reach agreement for whole generations' (Dowie 2001: 9). The third phase occurs some 25–30 years after the founder's death. In this stage the foundation is likely to be in the hands of complete strangers who are experts in the foundation's particular areas of interest. The fourth phase happens gradually as the number of foundation staff grows and the mode of operation becomes increasingly professionalised and bureaucratised. 'Preoccupied with their individual interests and institutions, the trustees increasingly defer in their decisions to the studies and recommendations of professional philanthrocrats' (Dowie 2001: 9). This pattern may or may not be fully applicable in the UK, but elements of it are certainly recognisable.

More generally, irrespective of the type and stage of the foundation, are trustees likely to be sources of innovation and renewal? Although we have no systematic data on the characteristics of foundation trustees, the impression is that they are predominantly middle-aged, male and from middle- or upper-class background. Many are members of 'the Great and the Good' and most are probably there because of past achievements rather than future promise. There is a plausible argument that foundations do not question or prod the system, not least because they are the system. Our analysis of the composition of trustee bodies of 100 of the top 300 foundations provides some limited support for this view. These 100 foundations had a total of 644 trustees of whom just over one-third (36.8 per cent) were female. Thirty-five per cent of these foundations had at least one titled member (for example, Lord, Baron).[9] We do not know how many are hereditary peers and how many appointed.member (for example, Lord, Baron).[10] We do not know how many are hereditary peers and how many appointed.

Foundation trustees (unless the deed specifies otherwise) are a self-perpetuating oligarchy. Existing trustees suggest potential new trustees, thus ensuring not only a narrow pool from which to draw but also consensus within the board. In some cases, there are only a handful of trustees. This 'law of sameness' is unlikely to generate the sort of conflict from which innovation often springs.

Trustees often suffer from another disadvantage: lack of time. Most trustees are already busy people—that, in a sense, is why they are selected in the first place—and have limited time to devote to the work of the foundation. This may mean that trustee meetings are relatively infrequent (perhaps quarterly) and of limited duration, sufficient to get

---

[9] This latter 'test' of the class of trustees is, of course, very severe. For example, it does not include many members of the Baring, Cadbury, Sainsbury, and other prominent families. A better measure would be the number of trustees listed in *Who's Who*.

[10] This latter 'test' of the class of trustees is, of course, very severe. For example, it does not include many members of the Baring, Cadbury, Sainsbury, and other prominent families. A better measure would be the number of trustees listed in *Who's Who*.

through the business in hand but not enough to engage in searching consideration of priorities, applications, or ways of working.

Some foundations clearly do change, identifying new priorities and ways of working. What is different about these foundations? One difference may be their type and stage in the life cycle. Another difference may be a deliberate policy of introducing new people, new ideas, and perhaps an element of conflict via the selection of new trustees. A tiny number of foundations appoint trustees for a fixed term. For example, BBC Children in Need trustees are appointed for a three-year term, whereas the Carnegie UK Trust appoints trustees for five years. Unusually, Carnegie UK has recently introduced a nominations committee, job specifications for trustees, vetting procedures, and advertisements for vacant positions (the latter also practised by, among a few others, Lloyds TSB Foundations). Another difference in innovative foundations may be the introduction of regular reviews of their work and a planning process that sees change as the norm rather than the exception.

## Staff

Paid staff are another potential source of change and renewal in foundations. Staff may bring new and different perspectives and knowledge of the social, political, economic, cultural, and technological changes in society that may be of interest to the foundation. In addition, the power relations between trustees and paid staff may be a source of constructive tension generating change and renewal in foundations. Although in the UK a relatively small proportion of foundations employ paid staff, most of the larger foundations do so. However, the power of staff undoubtedly varies widely between foundations ranging from a 'presidential' model, with most power vested in the position of the chief executive, to an 'administrator' model in which even the most senior staff merely administer the decisions of Trustees (Odendahl and Boris 1983; Odendahl et al, 1985). One indication of the power of staff relative to that of trustees may be their job titles. In the UK it is still possible to find staff with the title of 'secretary' or 'administrator', but titles such as 'director' and 'chief executive' are becoming more common.

We need research on how and why staff are appointed to foundations. What levels of pay are considered appropriate or necessary to attract suitably qualified people? What counts as 'qualified'? What skills are seen as necessary? Is there a developing career ladder within the foundation world such that staff move around and up within the sector? From what backgrounds do staff come? In the US the post of president or chief executive of a leading foundation is usually a reward for a distinguished career in academia, government, or business. In the UK this is rarely the case and the backgrounds of foundation directors appear to be varied. It is not clear whether staff are chosen as a result of a decision to bring new knowledge or change into the foundation, or whether the process works the other way about.

When staff are chosen for their expert knowledge of a particular field—for example, medicine, social services, the environment—they may indeed become a source of stability. Lack of flexibility is, in a sense, the other side of the coin of the knowledge that staff bring with them. 'A key staff appointment usually turns out to be a program decision, because a key staff appointment tends to set the framework of experience, intelligence, and imagination within which questions will be considered at staff level' (Dean Rusk quoted in Nason 1989: 78). More generally, there is a view that the professionalisation of foundations leads to bureaucratisation which seemingly stifles innovation. Foundations, it is alleged, can be truly innovative only when they retain a capacity for thinking and working 'out of the box', across the mind sets and disciplinary boundaries which professions represent.

A tiny minority of larger foundations now employ staff whose job description includes the monitoring of policy and other changes to inform the foundation's thinking about its roles, priorities, and ways of working. But there may be other sources of knowledge for change within foundations. Arguably grants officers in particular have large amounts of latent knowledge about what is happening in the fields in which the foundation operates, changes in the environment, and so on. However, few foundations have any systematic institutionalised means of tapping into this knowledge, and the 'transmission belt' for information to flow between grants officers and trustees is typically weak and underused. What is more, grants officers are usually fairly low in the foundation hierarchy.

**Consultants and advisers**

Historically, some of the most powerful figures in foundation giving have been those with knowledge rather than money: Frederick T. Gates, assistant to John D. Rockefeller Sr.; Donald Gallagher, religious adviser to Harry John of the De Rance Foundation; Robert Hutchins at the Ford Foundation; and a host of others. In the UK perhaps the most famous was Charles Dickens, who acted as adviser to Angela Burdett Coutts, the young heiress to the Coutts banking fortune and a major (and innovative) philanthropist.

Some of those who in the past were referred to as 'advisers' might now be termed 'paid staff' and incorporated into the core of the foundation structure; but ad hoc consultants and advisers are still used in foundations today instead of, or in addition to, paid staff. Consultants and advisers are typically involved in providing knowledge for investment of assets and for policy-making and grant-making. Those involved in advising in the initial stages of foundation formation and in investment of assets have received some attention (Ostrower 1987); but the selection and roles of those, sometimes influential, figures providing knowledge for grant-making have been relatively neglected (see Nielsen 1996).

Today, one reason for gaining the knowledge of consultants on an ad hoc basis is that it solves some of the problems associated with employing paid core staff. For example, it is argued that use of ad hoc consultants 'reduces the need for permanent staff and safeguards flexibility of program. Among small foundations with part-time or no staff, consultants can often serve the purpose of staff at lower cost' (Nason 1989: 81; see also Nason 1977).

But use of consultants may also create new problems. Apart from the difficulties in identifying the skills, knowledge, and experience needed by advisers and finding such people, there is likely to be a tension between disinterest and legitimacy. On the one hand, advisers must be knowledgeable in the field if they are to be accepted as credible and legitimate by both trustees and potential grant recipients. On the other hand, they must be disinterested. If a foundation does not consult those in a position to judge the quality of an application based on expert knowledge, they may be accused of arrogance, lack of understanding, and being out of touch with their constituencies, as well as running the risk of ineffective grant making. But if the foundation does consult such people they are likely to be accused of cronyism and self-dealing. Peer-group assessment, adopted by some research foundations as a means of acquiring expert knowledge and thus legitimacy, is rejected by others on the grounds that such methods not only encourage the formation of 'old boy networks' but also stifle innovation. Similar objections apply to the use of expert committees.

This tension between expert or 'insider' knowledge and disinterestedness is a continuing problem for many foundations today. Use of consultants to supplement knowledge may also create problems if trustees then feel that decisions are effectively taken out of their hands. Despite these difficulties and tensions it is clear that in some cases outside consultants do influence change in foundations in major ways, and more so during transition phases than in normal periods. Preparation for the appointment of a new director may trigger review and rethinking, and the new director himself (or, less likely, herself) may institute a review and change after his appointment.

Paradoxically, the recent vogue among larger foundations for strategic planning to achieve greater efficiency and effectiveness may have both encouraged and discouraged innovation. Strategic planning may encourage innovation within foundations in so far as it institutionalises change via encouragement of environmental scanning, regular review, proactive setting of priorities, and so on. But strategic planning may also discourage innovation in so far as it leaves little space for the truly new and unexpected, that is, aspects not anticipated in the strategic plan. Interestingly, one ex-director of a leading UK foundation has suggested that the system of quinquennial reviews undoubtedly encouraged innovation and renewal within the foundation but that its most innovative grant-making was the result of opportunistic responses to new issues not apparent at the time of the review (for example, responding to the needs of refugees and asylum seekers).

## Grant seekers and beneficiaries

In theory, grant seekers and beneficiaries are a—if not the—major source of change in foundations. In the past, and to a large extent still today in the UK, foundations engaged in reactive grant-making on the grounds that this ensured that they remained constantly in tune with changing needs in the community. However, given foundations' record in innovative grant-making, this has probably proved to be a somewhat unsatisfactory method of ensuring change within foundations. There are likely to be several reasons for this.

First, voluntary-sector grant seekers may not adequately reflect changing needs, partly because voluntary organisations themselves may be slow to change (especially perhaps larger organisations) and partly because newer organisations may not have the knowledge or skills to approach foundations. The various directories of trusts and foundations listed in *Directory of Social Change* contain an increasing number of comments from foundations that good-quality imaginative applications are becoming harder to find. Some foundations attribute this to voluntary organisations' increasing tendency to work on contract to local authorities (see, for example, comments by J. Paul Getty Charitable Trust in FitzHerbert, Forrester, and Grau 1997: 110). This criticism resonates well with the warning of Lord Dahrendorf (2001), who sees voluntary associations and foundations in danger of losing their innovative edge because of a governmental embrace that turns them into extended arms of the public sector.

Second, grant-seekers are very likely to give foundations what they think foundations want; thus, applications are likely to be tailored to what foundations have funded in the past rather than what they might fund in the future. For Adele Simmons, former president of the McArthur Foundation, foundations encourage 'institutionalised dishonesty' by which grant-seekers customise proposals to fit the foundation's priorities and interests in the hope of being able to cross-subsidise the real needs of the beneficiaries afterwards.[11] The overall result is a distorted 'grants economy' that operates on signals and symbols to maximise success rather than actual information about needs and ways to address problems on the ground.

Third, and closely related to the process of tailoring proposals, is the frequently off-putting language foundations use to discourage proposals outside their field. Indeed, foundations' greatest wrath is reserved for grant seekers who make applications outside stated priorities; in other words, applications which suggest, or might prompt, a process of change within the foundation are actively discouraged. Together, these three reasons make grant seekers, unlike customers in the business world, voters in politics, and users and members of voluntary organisations, ill-equipped to act as change agents in foundations.

---

[11] Presentation to the International Network of Strategic Philanthropy, Heidelberg, Germany, 22 March 2002.

Finally, the very processes of grant-seeking and grant-making, and the nature of the relationship between grant seekers and foundations, may discourage innovation. Grant-making is an inherently risky business for a variety or reasons, not the least of which is that grant makers cannot inspect the finished product in advance of giving a grant. The 'riskiness' of grant-making is one reason why trust is so important in the relationship between grant applicants/recipients and foundations. One ingredient in trust is reputation based on a proven track record. It is not surprising then that foundations tend to look favourably on grant applicants they have already funded or who have an established reputation (Leat 1998; Gronbjerg and Martell, with Paarlberg 2000). Indeed, this work suggests that 'insider' and 'outsider' applicants are treated very differently.

## Other foundations and funders

Within the foundation world there are no obvious mechanisms to ensure death or merger, let alone far-reaching adaptation. Unlike most other organisations, foundations exist in perpetuity; foundations may fade but they do not die (unless they choose to), nor are they 'prey to murder' by market mechanisms or the ballot box. Even when under threat they seem to have collective survival mechanisms; for example, during the passage of the 1969 Tax Act in the US there was a recommendation that US foundations should be limited to a 25-year life span, but foundations rallied to protect themselves and the recommendation was not passed (Troyer 2000; Dowie 2001).

In theory, as we suggested above, one might expect that one major source of change within the foundation world would be the entry of new foundations, as well as changes made by other foundations and funders.

Foundations claim that they fill gaps in existing provision and do what others don't do. Thus we would expect that, as foundation or funder A takes on funding in, say, social care, foundation B would change its priorities to focus on some other area of need. In fact, almost the opposite appears to be the case.

New foundations entering the foundation world might be expected to inject new blood, new thinking, and new practices. One problem here, however, may be that new private foundations tend to be started by people with similar values and from the same social strata as existing foundations (that is, those with particular pro-charitable attitudes from among the very wealthy, although there is an argument that the new rich are 'different'). In addition, it seems that some of those thinking of creating a new foundation tend to formulate their plans after consultation with existing foundations and influential law firms in the City of London. Both of these factors may encourage new foundations to reflect existing foundation cultures and practices.

Interestingly, and perhaps significantly, the National Lottery Boards may have had some effect on funding patterns in other foundations. The Lottery Boards did not come out of the usual social pool of foundation creators, and they had somewhat different constraints related to the circumstances of their birth, their source of income, and their political accountability. The sheer size of the Lottery Boards' grant-making capacity relative to that of other foundations meant that the effect they could create in the quiet foundation pond was less a matter or ripples and more akin to the potentially destabilising wash of a supertanker.

One element in the Lottery Boards' wash was the requirement (by some Boards) of matching funding before they would give a grant. This requirement, some foundations complained, was a form of blackmail forcing them to change their priorities in order to respond to the demands of grant applicants. Some existing foundations refused to change on principle. But whatever the effectiveness of the National Lottery Boards in encouraging change in foundations, this is probably a strategy only open to the very largest foundations.

At its worst, matching funding induces a false discipline, extending the pain of fund-raising for those who should be getting on with the job of innovating, often suppressing innovation altogether by capturing and emasculating the innovator. For some, matching funding has become a game in which intangible resources are allocated arbitrary financial values in order to meet the letter, if not the spirit, of requirements.

Other foundations may encourage change in fields other than grant-making priorities. The National Lottery Charities Board (now the Community Fund) is an interesting example here. NLCB, largely because of its public accountability, placed considerable emphasis on transparency, creating new application and assessment processes, as well as engaging in regular consultation and review. Arguably, NLCB has set new standards in grant-making processes as well as new models for other foundations to follow. It remains to be seen how many foundations will change their ways of working as a result; but the impression is that some larger and perhaps newer foundations are rethinking their practices in the light of the standards set by NLCB. (It could also be argued, however, that the Community Fund has been overly process driven, ignoring factors which might encourage creativity).

Institutional theory suggests that imitation is a powerful force for change (Powell and DiMaggio 1991). But institutional theory requires the existence of some sanctions. As noted above, the problem with applying institutional theory to endowed foundations is that there is no obvious sanction for failing to change. Sanctions do not, of course, need to be financial. Loss of reputation may be one non-financial sanction. But there are at least three problems in arguing that foundations are motivated to change through fear of loss of reputation. First, endowed foundations have no particular need to care about their reputations. Second, until recently there has been no mechanism for creation, and communication, of public reputation. Third, endowed foundations have traditionally ranked themselves in terms of their size or wealth rather than in terms of how they work or what they achieve.

The entry of new foundations, which do care about reputations because they are, or perceive themselves to be, publicly accountable, combined with publications which assess foundations by criteria other than wealth may have introduced new pressures for change in foundations along the lines suggested by institutional theory. A good example of the latter is the various directories published by the Directory of Social Change. The activities of the Association of Charitable Foundations to encourage interaction among foundations and to provide professional education and leadership may have added to these pressures, as did wider efforts such as the various Nolan reports that suggested new standards of what is acceptable in public life.

## Government

Over time the activities and priorities of government may be a trigger for change within individual foundations and the wider foundation sector. For example, in recent years changing statutory responsibilities are said to have placed new pressures on foundations, increasing levels of demand for grants and encouraging foundations to question their old perception of their role as 'doing what the state doesn't do' (Leat 1992).

In addition, recent governments have led foundations to rethink some of their funding processes and practices. For example, in the past foundations worked on the assumption that if they provided 'seed' funding a statutory funder would pay the longer-term bill. The principle was for foundations to provide short-term funding for demonstration projects, with successful project and practices to be supported by other, typically government, monies later. However, following an efficiency scrutiny of government funding of the voluntary sector in 1993, the then Conservative government announced that in future it would be providing short-term seed and demonstration funding, leaving others to pay the bill for longer-term support.

Government may also influence foundation priorities in other, less direct ways. For example, the New Labour government has invented such concepts as 'social exclusion' as well as pushing notions of 'civil society' and 'social capital' into wider public discourse and up the policy agenda. Some of the larger foundations appear to have adopted this language, although it remains to be seen whether this will lead to any noticeable change in their patterns of spending.

## Think tanks

Some foundations fund think tanks and other sources of generating new ideas, but it is unclear how much use they make of the organisations and ideas they fund in informing change within their own organisations. More likely are situations where foundations fund think tanks to influence policy-making more generally, and only indirectly the field of philanthropy. The Institute for Public Policy Research, Demos, the Policy Network, the Institute of Economic Affairs, and the New Economics Foundation, part funded by foundations, have on occasion ventured into the field of philanthropy, but not with the explicit charge to develop new policy models and practices.

## Constraints on Innovation/Renewal

The discussion above has suggested that foundations' interest in, and record of, innovation and renewal is far from clear, despite the frequent claim that innovation is one of their primary roles and virtues. Some part of the explanation for foundations' apparent failure to live up to their own claims must lie in the way in which foundations choose, or don't choose, to operate. But there are other factors over which foundations have less control that present constraints on innovation and renewal in foundations.

## The trust deed

The trust deed is one constraint on change within foundations. Some trust deeds, especially ones created more recently, have broad purposes, which allow wide scope for reinterpretation in the light of changing circumstances. Some foundation creators tie the foundation to fairly narrow purposes but have the prescience to realise that they cannot foresee all eventualities and build into the foundation scope and responsibility for change. Joseph Rowntree is probably the most famous example of the latter approach.  As discussed above, when the foundation deed is drawn narrowly it may very quickly become outdated or inappropriate, for a variety of reasons. In these cases, change can in theory be achieved via the legal *cy près* rule. But apart from the time and complexity and cost involved in this route, it can prove unsatisfactory as a vehicle for change.

The Buck Trust case in the US in the 1980s illustrates the unforeseen ways in which a foundation deed may quickly become of questionable relevance and the limitations of the *cy près* rule in remedying this. Beryl Buck's fortune was held largely in oil shares. When she made her will creating a foundation she believed she was worth around $5 million. The foundation she created was to be concerned solely with assisting the poor in her home region: Marin County, California, the second richest county in the US. By the time Mrs Buck died her estate, and thus the foundation, was worth $200 million. Faced with the virtual impossibility of sensibly spending the income on $200 million on 'the poor' in such an affluent area, and the very real and pressing needs in adjacent areas, the Trustees applied to the courts to alter the foundation's mission to take in a wider geographical area than that specified by Mrs Buck, arguing both that it would be philanthropically irresponsible to spend this amount of money in such an affluent area and that Mrs Buck had not intended to leave $200 million for this purpose. The courts rejected the Trustees request.

The effects of restrictions on change of purpose of charitable foundations need examination, balancing the need for regular modernisation with the need to maintain the confidence of donors and potential donors that their wishes will be respected. We regard the law and practice of *cy près* as a prime area of regulatory reform in this field, and generally opt for broader and modernising interpretations of the original deed under *cy près* conditions.

## Charity law and the Charity Commission

More generally, charity law and the Charity Commission exist primarily to maintain and protect the status quo rather than for the purpose of encouraging change. In particular, charity law and the Charity Commission must balance protection of the rights and wishes of donors with calls for change and flexibility. In recent years, the Charity Commission has nonetheless demonstrated a new taste for change by, for example, changing trust deeds and extending its interpretation of 'charitable purposes', view supported by the Cabinet Office (2002: 36-42). The Cabinet Office favours a broader range of public benefit purposes, and recommends the Charity Commission to undertake on-going checks on the public character of charitable activities.

But it cannot be the purpose of the Charity Commission to regulate the innovative pursuit of public benefit, and it is open to debate to what extent the Charity Commission should rule over internal affairs of foundations. Should the law the periods of service for trustees, or their characteristics (other than some basic minimum requirements barring those with criminal convictions, and so on), or the need for regular renewal of trustees? The continuing freedom of foundations to work as stable and self-perpetuating oligarchies contrasts with most statutory funding bodies, which now have maximum periods of appointment of no more than a few years for trustees. Similarly, as already mentioned, the law in Britain does not require foundations to make any minimum level of annual payout.

Neither the law nor the Commission has anything to say on the need for institutionalised channels for change and renewal. For example, there is no requirement for regular independent review or similar forms of assessment. Lack of any legal requirements, or regulatory framework, encouraging change does nothing to counter foundations' cultural and organisational resistance to the 'ingredients' of change. Indeed, some see the Charity Commission as the single biggest obstacle to innovation and in need of urgent reform, particularly in splitting its executive and judiciary functions. While it is true that the roles of regulator and 'friend' are a difficult combination, arguably the Commission's general approach is a symptom rather than a cause of the complacency of politicians, and wider society, regarding charitable foundations. Legal and regulatory changes alone seem very unlikely to be sufficient to promote creativity.

In "Private Action, Public Benefit" the Cabinet Office (2002: 71-89) clarifies the role of the Charity Commission and specifies that the Commission "should review, with sector participation, and report on the performance of different charitable sub-sectors with a view to correcting information failures and enabling stakeholders to maximise beneficiaries' interests and better fulfil underlying charitable objects" (2002: 81). We see this as the first steps into the right direction. Having a regular review of foundations (as a charitable sub-sector) that enlists different views, identifies strengths and weaknesses across the field in terms of information management, operations, activities, performance and impact, could be an important element in creating the debate about the role of foundations we see so clearly lacking in this country.

# Conclusion

The discussion above suggests that for a variety of reasons foundations are ill-equipped to foster innovation. Foundations are sometimes presented as bastions of conservatism, congenitally disposed to resist change. There may be some truth in this view but an equally plausible suggestion may be that foundations fail to champion change not so much because they are against change per se but rather because they lack, for structural reasons, the drive and knowledge to conceive of better ways of promoting the public good. Yet, even if we argued that foundations were predisposed to foster social change and innovation, and that they had the knowledge and imagination to pursue these goals, are they likely to be successful?

The theories of social change and innovation with which foundations work are unclear, if indeed they are consciously formulated at all. On the surface at least many foundations' assumptions about how social change is achieved appear extraordinarily naive. Social change and innovation seem very unlikely to be achieved by giving small, and often inadequate, amounts of money for a very short period to large numbers of relatively powerless organisations unschooled and ill-resourced in communications and marketing and without channels of policy influence. But this is exactly what many UK foundations do.[12]

---

[12] It is worth noting here that the Joseph Rowntree Foundation estimates that it has taken 14 years of continuous effort (as well as a sophisticated dissemination and marketing strategy) to achieve a significant policy change in at least one of its areas of interest (interview with former trustee) achieve a significant policy change in at least one of its areas of interest (interview with former trustee).

It is also worth noting that in recent years in the US some of the most successful foundations in terms of achieving social change have been right-wing foundations (National Committee for Responsive Philanthropy, NCRP, 1997). These foundations have adopted a very different approach from their 'liberal' peers by spending large amounts of money on building institutions rather than programmes. 'And since conservatives don't continually shift program priorities, conservative organisations don't have to repackage their agenda or scramble to replace old funding with new' (Karen Paget quoted in Dowie 2001: 216). Rather than adopting the 'fund it and forget it' approach of many of their peers, conservative foundations have emphasised communications, marketing, and constituency development as essential elements in achieving effective change. This approach is now being adopted by other UK and US foundations (see, for example, Lake, Reis, and Spann 2000).

We return to the issues of innovation, development, and renewal in the final chapter. In the following chapter we consider key elements in the changing context in which foundations work: the context that constrains or extends the role foundations can play, and that sets the scene for consideration of a new, more clearly articulated vision for the sector as a whole. We also look briefly at new forms of philanthropy and their relationship to this changing context.

# Chapter 4

# Foundations in a Changing Context

*Helmut K. Anheier and Diana Leat*

# Introduction

So far we have looked at foundations in a somewhat static perspective. Yet one of the observations we made in Chapter 1 was that the world around philanthropy has changed more than philanthropy itself. We argued that what was once a highly innovative element of modern society, namely, the development of the philanthropic foundation, now stands in danger of falling behind its promise. In this chapter, we identify a range of threats and opportunities that foundations must address if they are to move beyond the remnants of 19th-century philanthropic paternalism to create new visions and renewed legitimacy in the 21st century. We begin by taking a closer look at the changes in the environment in which foundations operate, and then consider developments within the foundation world, in particular the rise of the 'new' philanthropies.

# Changes in the Environment

For reasons we outlined in previous chapters, endowed foundations are less subject to external pressures than most other types of organisation. Nevertheless, they operate in economic, social, political, and cultural environments from whose pressures they are not totally immune and to which, arguably, they need to respond. We suggested that such a response is needed if foundations are to maintain and even rebuild some of the legitimacy they enjoy and require.

This section identifies some recent changes in the environment in which foundations operate and the ways in which these have affected foundations. Some of the factors outlined below impact directly on foundations; others are more relevant to operating charities, but have an indirect effect on foundations in setting the scene in which foundations and their recipients work.


## Increasing income

In recent years some foundations have enjoyed spectacular increases in income due in part to booming property and investment values and in part to the proceeds of takeovers and mergers. Even though the recent fall in stock market values has decreased the assets of some foundations, their combined net worth is still significantly higher than before the boom of the 1990s.


## Increasing tax benefits

Although foundations have suffered tax losses in recent years, concern with the efficiency and effectiveness of foundations has to be seen in the wider context of increasing tax benefits, particularly in the light of the 2001 tax incentives for charitable giving in the UK. As the scope and scale of taxation have grown the value of the tax advantages enjoyed by charities has also increased. This is likely to have two effects. First, as charitable status becomes more financially valuable there is likely to be greater concern to bestow this status more carefully and to police it more effectively. Second, as the sums of 'lost' public revenue grow there is likely to be greater concern regarding the use of such monies.[13]

---

[13] In the US growing concerns about private inurnment (the use of the non-profit form for private gain) led to passing of the Taxpayers' Bill of Rights 1996 which gives the IRS sanctions in the form of penalty taxes on organisations which violate the private inurnment rules (Salamon 1997: 41; Troyer 2000).

## Cultures of efficiency and effectiveness

One of the most profound changes in the last 20 years has been the culture of efficiency and effectiveness introduced to the public and voluntary sector by the Thatcher administrations (see Ferlie 1996). All service provision receiving public funding, including that provided by charities, is now assessed (in theory at least) in terms of its efficiency and effectiveness. Interestingly, and perhaps significantly, these pressures have not been explicitly applied to foundations enjoying the benefits of tax expenditures rather than direct subsidy. But within this wider culture many foundations have begun to look at their own operations in a new light, questioning both the efficiency and effectiveness of their activities.[14]

## Changing public expectations and new standards in public life

Concern with efficiency and effectiveness—seen in market terms as business values—was followed by new, or revived, emphasis on standards of behaviour and governance in public life. In a number of countries the late 1990s saw heavily publicised scandals in government and corporate life, leading to efforts to redefine and reassert expectations of acceptable conduct. In the UK the Cadbury Committee on corporate governance and the Nolan Committee on standards in public life were just two examples of this new concern with standards. Fortunately, there have been no UK equivalents of the scandals shocking US philanthropy: for example, the United Way scandal or the demise of New Era Philanthropy and similar Ponzi schemes.

---

[14] There are some interesting questions here regarding the routes by which this culture permeated foundations. Arguably what is surprising is not that this happened but that it had not happened before, given the dominance of men of business on the boards of foundations.

**Demands for greater accountability and transparency**

Concern with standards in public life, coupled with various other factors discussed above and below, fed demands for greater accountability and transparency. The non-profit sector, so long regarded by many as a repository of trust, has not completely escaped demands for greater accountability. Statutory funders and purchasers, as well as voluntary and corporate funders, are requiring new forms of accountability, and other demands for greater accountability come from users (see Plowden 2001).

In the US and the UK in particular, media attention has led to questions about issues ranging from salaries to reserves to poor-quality, and in some cases positively damaging, services (Fleishman 1999). Throughout the world, there have been various recent scandals concerning fraud and misappropriation of funds within non-profit organisations, including foundations. As yet, the issue of voluntary sector accountability has not attracted the popular attention devoted to accountability in the private and public sectors.

Arguably, complacency rather than corruption is the real problem in the UK foundation world. Foundation governance and accountability (as in the wider non-profit sector) have traditionally been based on assumptions about purity and probity derived largely from organisational form and lack of a profit motive. The assumption has been that such organisations would 'behave well' precisely because their motives and goals were altruistic (see Rose-Ackerman 1996). In addition to informal assumptions and expectations foundation governance and accountability have been based on certain legal requirements. These include charity law, company law, tax law, and other legislation relating to specific organisations/charities and specific areas of activity.

In recent years, the Guides to Grant Making Trusts published by the Directory of Social Change (see, for example, Fitzherbert and Eastwood 1989; Fitzherbert and Richards 2001) have dramatically increased the accountability of foundations by naming and shaming those failing to provide adequate information on their spending activities. Changes in the law and recommended accounting practices for charities (including foundations) have further increased demands for accountability (see Cabinet Office 2002). In the last five years, a growing number of trusts and foundations throughout the world, via their associations, have developed codes of good practice, including the European Foundation Centre in Brussels.

## Corporate giving

Some of the factors mentioned above have contributed to a new concern with corporate responsibility, which, in turn, has created new relationships between business and philanthropic organisations (see, for example, Burlingame and Young 1996; Himmelstein 1997; Elkington 1998). In some countries, foundations have become conduits for corporate giving of shareholders' money. Sensitivity to demonstrating probity, as well as efficiency and effectiveness, in all of their activities has led business to expect similar standards of the foundations they have created, as well as those non-profit organisations with which they work.

## Ethical investment

Allied to a concern with corporate responsibility there have been pressures from consumers, shareholders, and others for 'ethical investment' by large businesses in particular. Foundations have not been immune from these wider pressures for ethical investment. Indeed, some foundations see themselves as having a special imperative to pursue the same goals and values in their investment decisions as they do in their grant-making. Joseph Rowntree Charitable Trust, for example, has been a leading player in getting the ethical investment movement of the ground in the UK. Increasingly, how foundations invest their considerable assets may come under as much scrutiny as how they spend their money (for developments in the US see Dowie 2001).

## Professionalism and managerialism

Partly in response to some of the trends above, non-profit organisations, including foundations, have increasingly employed paid professional, technical, and general managerial staff (Kramer 1990; Bruce and Leat 1993; Brown, Kenny, and Turner, 2000). On the one hand, this may be seen as a way of making foundations and other non-profit organisations better managed and more accountable. But, at the same time, the growth of paid professional staff within foundations creates new tensions.

For one, the introduction of paid professional managers creates a separation between policy-making and policy implementation, which in turn raises issues of governance and accountability for 'appropriate' or 'adequate' implementation. If, in addition, those employed to manage the organisation and to implement policy claim some professional competence then governance and accountability take on a new and potentially troublesome dimension; the role of the management committee must be reconciled in theory and in practice with the claims of managers and employees to professional authority and autonomy. Of course, these problems are not peculiar to non-profit organisations but may be of special significance in so far as governance by independent volunteer trustees has been considered a defining characteristic (on the issue of definition see, for example, Salamon and Anheier 1997). Paid professional staff may, as we have discussed in the previous chapter, also introduce a new 'inflexibility' in the way foundations operate in their areas of interest, a concern most clearly voiced by Karl and Katz (1981).

Moreover, professionalism and managerialism within foundations may sit uneasily with the wider cultural emphasis on user involvement. Like the business and public sectors, non-profit organisations have been subject to demands that the end user, the consumer, be taken into account. The growth of consumerism has led to changes in the internal structure and culture of some non-profit organisations, as well as a change in the overall shape and character of the sector as a whole, as new organisations started by consumers for consumers have joined the ranks of older, more paternal organisations.

Some foundations have responded to this movement by including end users in decision-making structures and processes. Others have responded by giving priority to grant applications from 'user-led' organisations. This may not only increase the complexity of decision making and appropriate accountability from grant recipients but may also raise questions about the governance and accountability models and practices of foundations more generally. Some ask: if foundations require user involvement in their grant recipients, should they not practise what they preach? This has raised wider questions about the congruence in governance and accountability between what foundations require of others and of themselves.

## Public trust and confidence

The growth of professionalism and managerialism within the non-profit sector may have also contributed, along with other factors above, to loss of public trust and confidence in the sector. In various countries, there is growing evidence of a loss of public trust and confidence in non-profit organisations including trusts and foundations. In part, this loss of confidence has been generated by scandals within the sector including the New Era, United Way, and other scandals in the US. Having chosen the moral high ground by presenting themselves as 'the value led sector', non-profit organisations are now being required to produce evidence of their trustworthiness.

Specific scandals within non-profit organisations have largely been explained as the acts of individual rogues rather than an indication of deeper structural problems. Nevertheless, the fact that rogues have been able to operate undetected for significant periods of time has led to questions regarding the adequacy of non-profit organisation governance and accountability structures and processes (Ilchman and Burlingame 1999).

Specific scandals aside, there is growing evidence in the US and UK of a more general loss of confidence in non-profit organisations (Salamon 1997; Henley Centre 1998). In part, this lack of confidence has been fuelled by the right: 'Conservative critics have come to recognise the significant role that nonprofit organisations have played in surfacing public problems and mobilising support for their resolution. Rather than applauding this crucial advocacy function of nonprofit organisations as a sign of the vibrancy of American democracy, however, they deplore it as a potent mechanism for fuelling the continued growth of the modern welfare state' (Salamon 1997). This critique is enforced by the overt political role some foundations play in policy development and in the way political discourse is being shaped. The role of the conservative foundations in the US in forging the 'Washington Consensus' of neo-liberalism is a key example here (see Dowie 2001).

This loss of public trust and confidence in the sector is matched by growing questioning in academic theory and research of the characteristics of non-profit organisations. Traditionally, non-profit organisations including foundations have claimed for themselves certain virtues and functions including a capacity for innovation, greater cost effectiveness and flexibility, greater efficiency, greater understanding of users, lack of bureaucracy, greater democracy, and so on. These virtues have largely been taken for granted despite the lack of systematic empirical evidence to support them. More recently academic research has begun to question the basis for such claims (for a summary, see for example: McIlnay 1998; Flynn and Hodgkinson 2002). Furthermore, with the growing emphasis on business standards and models non-profits are increasingly measured against these and found wanting (Fleishman 1999).

**Europe**

The vast majority of UK foundations have traditionally taken little interest in funding beyond Britain. Indeed, most exclude any 'foreign' funding. Given that many of the major social issues in Britain today have a European dimension, and that the locus of debate for much policy- and law-making is now in both Brussels and Westminster, foundations may find it increasingly difficult to maintain a purely domestic approach. Our membership of the European Union has potentially profound implications for foundations to which very little thought appears to have been given to date. Few UK foundations are members of the European Foundation Centre, although that may say as much about perceived relevance of the EFC as it does about UK foundations' interest in Europe.

## Globalisation

Globalisation of markets is widely regarded as reducing the power of the nation state and politicians, and at same time as encouraging the development of local communities, local cultural identities and nationalisms, and a return to forms of local democracy in which the public sector is no longer identified solely with the state (see, for example, Giddens 2001). Fuzzy sovereignty means multiple identities and multiple allegiances requiring a more tolerant society.

According to Giddens (2001), globalisation implies a more active citizenry with old-style voluntary organisations becoming less important and new-style partly professionalised self-help groups becoming more important, and with new roles for third-sector organisations in community renewal, social entrepreneurship, and 'activating social capital'. The new 'effort bargain' gives third-sector groups a more direct role in government and the formation of government policy in return for greater efficiency, effectiveness, and accountability. The effects on foundations of these challenges are, as yet, unclear (see below). While some US foundations have long been global actors, and more are in the process of looking if not operating across borders (Renz 1997; Anheier and List 2000), relatively few UK foundations have reacted to globalisation in terms of funding patterns (see Pinter 2001).

## New policies, new roles

The effects of globalisation are part of the potentially most far-reaching change in the environment of foundations: redefinition of the role of the state in pursuit of public benefit. In the UK and other European countries, as well as in the US and Australia, there is growing acceptance that the state is incapable of dealing with social, economic, and environmental issues alone. 'The Third Way' (Giddens 1998), social coalition, cross-sector alliances and partnerships are now central policy tenets (see contributions in Anheier 2001). The metaphor of government as 'steering not rowing' and the associated growth of contracting out creates new and complex dilemmas in relationships between organisations involved in pursuit of public benefit (Salamon and Anheier 1996; Anheier and Kendall 2001).

Foundations exist to pursue public benefit; so, too, does government. But the relationship between foundations and government has always been, to a degree, contentious. Foundations in the UK have traditionally presented themselves as independent of government, operating in areas 'beyond' the state, doing what the state doesn't do, while at the same time behaving in ways which directly or indirectly impact on government. This is the traditional role of foundations as supplement and gap-filler to government action.

In recent years this position has been challenged in various direct and indirect ways. As the old consensus regarding statutory responsibilities broke down in the 1980s, foundations found 'doing what the state doesn't do' an increasingly unsatisfactory guide to policy and practice. At the same time, government turned the tables on foundations (and charities in general), expecting them to play a larger role in funding and provision of public benefit as well as taking on the role of 'pilot' funder leaving foundations to pay the bill for longer-term funding, as we argued in the previous chapter.

The New Labour government developed this new 'vision' of foundations' roles with the notion of the Third Way and heavy use of the term 'partnership' (see Mulgan 2001; Deakin 2001; Bennington 2001; Dahrendorf 2001). Although this puts a more friendly gloss on foundation relationships with government, it does little to clarify roles and relationships. Furthermore, the notion that foundations can and should 'take up the slack' still lurks beneath the surface, playing 'around the relation between foundations and government like Casper the Friendly Ghost, obviously eager to be loving and sociable, but surprised at the alarm he seems to raise' (Karl and Karl 1999: 66).

The creation of the New Opportunities Fund as a separate and more directly controlled body than the Community Fund (previously National Lottery Charities Board) working to government priorities is seen by some as further evidence of takeover by stealth. Similarly, community foundations, dispensing local grants on behalf of government, are discovering that working under contract to government sometimes feels like a very unequal partnership with implications for ways of working, priorities, costs, and accountability.

Given that 'The Third Way is not a doctrine, a blueprint or fixed ideology, but rather, a work in progress' (Mulgan 2001: 21), the meaning of the Third Way remains unclear as a general policy principle. However, there appear to be four areas in which the Third Way and the third sector come into close proximity (Anheier 2000).

First, under the Third Way, policy-making and governance are no longer the primary and final responsibility of government. Instead, they are shared with other agencies including non-profit organisations. Second, the Third Way and the third sector are related via the concept of civil society in which non-profit organisations play a crucial role. The third and fourth areas of contact are the social economy and social welfare. The Third Way emphasises the public responsibility of private economic action and with it the role of social economy institutions such as cooperatives, mutuals, and non-profits (see Yeo 2002). The Third Way implies a redefinition of social welfare and reorganisation of financing and delivery with the third sector becoming part of this new economy (see Anheier 2002; Deakin 2001).

The implications of the above have been delineated by the Cabinet Office for the voluntary sector as a whole (2002: 32), but the specificities for foundations remain unclear: for the roles and responsibilities of foundations, for their relationships with the state and those they fund, for their funding priorities and practices, for who is funded (for example, semi-statutory organisations), for the terms of co-funding relationships, for accountability of grant recipients to foundations and foundations' accountability to the state. At the least, new policy approaches have required rethinking of how foundations relate to the state. Government has redesigned its own pitch, and 'team', and expects foundations to play along. The old foundation mantras—'Doing what the state doesn't do', and/or 'Doing what the state isn't responsible for doing', 'filling gaps', and so on—are no longer acceptable, or workable, game rules.

Emphasis on partnerships between public, private, and non-profit organisations, and the creation of hybrid organisations, have broken down the old divisions between sectors, creating new dilemmas for foundations in deciding when a grant becomes a subsidy to government or business—and whether that matters. 'Partnerships' have also directly and indirectly created new pressures on foundations for provision of matching funding, which some foundations see as a threat to their autonomy in choice of priorities, as we suggested in the case of the Community Fund above.

Growing privatisation of provision has added to pressures for accountability of non-profit organisations, not merely because such organisations may be in receipt of larger sums of state funding. More significantly, such pressure arises because, instead of providing the 'extras', non-profit organisations are now regarded as central players in the provision of services for which governments now merely 'contract' and accept some overall responsibility.

Greater demands for accountability from government funders have largely taken the form of contracts for service. These have not only increased and formalised accountability responsibilities but also created tensions in some organisations. These tensions have concerned the appropriateness of government funders' accountability demands, criteria, and processes; relationships with accountability to other stakeholders, including foundation funders; and effects on internal governance. One wider effect has been to raise questions about the accountability and governance of all non-profit organisations, whether on contract or not. In some cases, foundations have been asking more detailed questions of those they fund, which in turn has led to greater self-scrutiny.

More generally various nagging questions remain including (Anheier 2000):

- 'Who determines the appropriate roles for government, the voluntary sector, and business?

- Do differences in power and legitimacy no longer matter? Who designs and oversees future partnerships involving the third sector?

- Who decides what accountability means for whom, to whom, and for what end?

- Should values be shared? What if the values of voluntary sector groups and government do not coincide? Who decides which values are shared and which ones not?

These questions suggest various potential roles for foundations. Foundations could play a greater role in policy-making. Foundations could take advantage of their independence to address and referee the difficult issues in identifying the terms on which there can be partnerships of mutual benefit between government, the corporate sector, and the and voluntary sector. Foundations could ensure the survival of an independent alternative voluntary sector that does not simply follow government's agenda. Given that the policy preference for private institutions serving public purposes comes at a time when the very notion and content of the collective good is being contested, foundations could play an important, independent, 'apolitical' role in promoting debate about a new understanding of the collective good. In fulfilling these roles, as we discuss in the next chapter, real creativity is crucial.

Finally, the new emphasis on the role of non-profit organisations in creating social capital and in providing the infrastructure of civil society has, on the one hand, provided a new (and difficult to validate in empirical terms) rationale for supporting such organisations. On the other hand, the emphasis on social capital and civil society sits somewhat uneasily with some foundations' new desire for focus, efficiency, and effectiveness. Given that the social capital and civil society rationales attach considerable significance to the democratic styles and functions of non-profit organisations, participation, governance and accountability, and 'localness' are of potentially greater importance than other more measurable outputs.

## The New Philanthropists/Philanthropies

How has the foundation world changed in recent years? To what extent do the new philanthropists and styles of philanthropy address the environmental changes and demands on foundations outlined above?

### Community foundations

Already well-established in the US, community foundations are relatively new to the UK and are one of the fastest foundation growth areas in recent years. There are now over 30 established community foundations and a further 30 at various stages of development. In 2000, the 29 best-established community foundations held £92 million in endowments and made grants totalling £21.9 million. Community foundations describe themselves as helping to build and strengthen the capacity of local communities through: [15]

- 'constructive local grant-making for voluntary and community activity;

- the building of endowment to create permanent community capital;

- the encouragement of local philanthropy;

- being a vehicle for donors' charitable interests; and

- acting as a catalyst in local initiatives.'

In the UK and Europe, growth of community foundations has been fuelled by grants from US foundations including the Charles Stewart Mott Foundation, the Ford Foundation, and the MacArthur, Lilly, and Kellogg foundations. In some countries community foundation development has been based on transposing a US model based on certain American and 'capitalist' assumptions to economies and cultures where these are of dubious relevance (for example, stable stock markets; in other countries, such as Germany, foundations like the Bertelsmann Stiftung developed new models more applicable to local circumstances and cultures (Bertelsmann Foundation 1999b).

---

[15] Information based on private correspondence with representatives of the Community Foundation Network in London.

In many respects, community foundations are ideally suited to the new policy environment we described above. They are rooted in, and emphasise building, local communities; they encourage and provide vehicles for corporate giving; they are governed locally; they encourage citizen-donor involvement and 'democratise' giving by enabling smaller donors to create what are, in effect, their own mini-foundations (for example, donor-advised funds) within an established infrastructure; and they seek to work with rather than apart from local government and businesses.

But community foundations need to meet the criticisms of parochialism in multicultural societies, of failing to recognise the tension between local public good and public good at the level of the nation state, of increasing disparities between communities by providing another resource to those wealthy areas which can afford to create them; encouraging lack of coordination by allowing donor-advised funds, encouraging donor control and whims and fancies; and further undermining democratically elected local government by setting themselves up as forums for debate of social issues.

In the US there have been various reports critical of community foundations. The NCRP (2000) compared community foundations and alternative funds. Alternative funds primarily raise contributions from employees at the workplace and have not benefited from foundation investments of the sort enjoyed by US (and UK) community foundations: 'with 25-30 times more foundation investment over time, community foundations only manage to make grants three times the size of alternative fund distributions ($2.3 million compared to $692,000 per alternative fund).' The usual counter to this sort of criticism is that endowment-building institutions like community foundations are important for long-term community development; but alternative funds often provide stable operating expenses for their members.

Other criticisms point to the elitist nature of current philanthropy: 'philanthropic paternalism that vests much of the influence over the definition of community needs in the hands of those in command of the greatest resources' (Salamon 1987). In a similar vein, it is argued that the need to compete for donor support means that the predominant role of nonprofits is to provide the services and amenities communities prefer rather than to act as a charitable agent (Wolpert, 1995). If applied to community foundations these criticisms would lead one to expect that community foundations would function as elite-serving or distributive, not redistributive, institutions. This sits uncomfortably with community foundations' presentation of themselves as 'comprised of public spirited, grass roots institutions which possess a unique capability to respond to the most pressing community problems' (www.ncrp.org/reports).

Questions about community foundations responsiveness to the most pressing social needs are underlined by another report from the NCRP (1991), which found that this community foundation's activities benefited the disadvantaged only 'willy nilly, not as part of any deliberate plan'. Of the California Community Foundation's $9.3 million grants in 1989 only 22 per cent went to benefit disadvantaged and disenfranchised people. The Foundation was found to have high tolerance for failure and low tolerance for social change; it was not inclined to fund organisations promoting private or public policy change to improve the lives of disadvantaged people

Partly because of these criticisms of community foundations in the US, some new philanthropists have aligned themselves with 'community-based' philanthropy as distinct from community foundations.

## Community-based philanthropy

- 'Community-based philanthropic organisations are (or strive to be):

- Accountable—practising honesty and transparency and answering to a wider community

- Compassionate—being motivated to alleviate the suffering of others

- Inclusive—valuing all people equally and treating people with respect regardless of their race, culture, religion, language, immigration, history, age, class, sexual orientation, gender or disabilities

- Democratic—involving a broad range of constituencies in decision making processes

- Strategic—addressing root causes of social, economic and environmental problems, often with innovative and creative approaches

- Collaborative—working in partnership with like-minded organisations and building bridges between donors and grantees' (from http://www.changemakers.net/).

Again there is an emphasis on 'partnerships', consultation, and accountability. Community-based philanthropy appears to attempt to distinguish itself from community foundations by emphasising its wider range of constituencies and its strategic approach, and by not mentioning endowment building or donor control.

**Proactive philanthropy**

Whereas foundations have traditionally emphasised their reactivity—reacting or responding to the 'priorities' expressed by the spread of grant applications—new styles of philanthropy tend to be more openly and assertively proactive, actively seeking out applications for undertaking the work which they have identified as a priority. Proactive philanthropy is often allied with an emphasis on 'strategic' grant-making.

**Strategic philanthropy**

The term 'strategic philanthropy' appears to have originated in the corporate sector where it is most often used to refer to giving which fits with wider company strategy. The term is now used more broadly with a variety of meanings.

One common meaning is to 'moving away from grant-making as an end in itself, and beginning to think about developing strategies to solve problems seeing grants as pieces of activity that implement strategy' (Gaberman 1999). A report by the Pew Charitable Trust lists ten criteria for strategic philanthropy (Rimel, 1999):

1. Well defined goal

2. Discernible impact on a problem

3. Responds to a ripe opportunity and is timely

4. Has appropriate partnerships

5. Is simply in design

6. Allocates an appropriate amount of resources

7. Approaches a problem on multiple fronts

8.  Is ambitious yet feasible

9.  Considers core competencies, internal as well as external

10. Aims to show progress in three to five years.

We find much to recommend about strategic philanthropy, as we do about venture philanthropy below. At the same time, we feel that it lacks a broader vision and conceptual grounding for foundations, and that brings their central competencies into focus. In other words, strategic philanthropy, while the right step in to the right direction, is not 'radical' enough, and has, unfortunately, too easily become a diffuse term used to refer to:

- funding or other grant-making or giving which is proactive rather than reactive, that is, which seeks to initiate or encourage particular types of organisation or work rather than simply reacting to applications from existing organisations; and

- funding which is designed to bring about desired social change often through new approaches and methods; and/or which emphasises certain values such as social justice and structural change.

**Progressive philanthropy/grant-making**

Progressive philanthropy is usually contrasted with 'traditional charitable giving' to refer to grant-making based on a commitment to a just and inclusive society, with grants given to improve the circumstances of people with limited choices and resources.

## Venture philanthropy

Venture philanthropy is one of the most fashionable 'new' styles of philanthropy, although how it differs exactly from some 'older' forms of grant-making is not entirely clear.

'Venture philanthropy refers to the nonprofit sector's application of certain practices used by venture capitalists when investing in new business ideas' (Center for Venture Philanthropy URL). Venture philanthropy may also be used more loosely to refer to all kinds of charitable endeavours that involve risk-taking, innovation, and entrepreneurship. Specifically, it includes 'funding social entrepreneurs in organisations with scale-up potential. Support it long term and the funder makes substantial commitments to a few rather than smaller commitments to many' (Reis and Clohesy, 2001: 477).

A report by the Roberts Foundation under the leadership of Jed Emerson (Emerson and Twersky, 1996), and an article in the *Harvard Business Review* article by Letts, Ryan, and Grossman (1997), titled 'Virtuous Capital: What Foundations Can Learn from Venture Capital', are regarded as the venture philanthropy manifestos. They criticise foundations for investing in programmes and projects rather than non-profit infrastructure, capacity building, and entrepreneurial talent. Letts, Ryan, and Grossman (1997) urge foundations to borrow six strategies from venture capitalists: deploying risk management tools, creating performance measures, developing close relationships with their investments, investing more money, investing over longer periods, and developing an exit strategy.

The development of venture philanthropy is associated with new and younger donors who know the systems to which they are being asked to contribute and know the defects. Like some donors to community foundations, venture philanthropists still want to be able to control their wealth even in the act of giving. But the venture capital model takes donor control a step further, involving participation in governance and management of funded organisations. The language and culture of venture philanthropy is that of the business world: grants become equity, funders are investors, grantees are investees, and proposals become business plans.

Venture philanthropy is a radical departure from the genteel world of foundation boardrooms. Its dual emphasis on 'value for money and money for value', and its interest in developing the notion of 'value' in non-profit capital markets are bold steps forward. At the very least, the introduction of venture philanthropy has broadened the options available to donors; at its best, it is the initial step to go beyond the philanthropic foundation that has now been the dominant model for a century.

For us, the question is less whether to reject venture philanthropy wholesale, as some critics have done, but rather to ask if indeed, the model offered has the potential to develop into the new way of philanthropy generally: form 19th century charity, and 20th century organised, grant-making philanthropy, to 21st century venture philanthropy. Our assessment is that, for reasons pointed out below, venture philanthropy is unlikely to emerge as 'the' model of the modern foundation. At the same time, the 21st century foundation will have many elements of the ideas developed by Emerson as well as by Letts and her colleagues.

Venture philanthropy is much less organisation-based than 20th century philanthropy has been and continues to be. To some extent, one does not need foundations at all—an individual with disposable financial means ready to invest on the one hand, and an individual with a sellable idea and worked out business plan are all what is needed. The instrument of the deed, the institution of trusteeship and narrower legal notions of charity and public benefit no longer matter, at least to the extent to which they do in conventional foundations.

Is this a problem? At one level it is not, as venture philanthropy sees itself as a break with the past—albeit one that turns the idea of private action for public benefit into a variant of the business venture. At another level it is problematic for three reasons: first, while venture philanthropy attaches great significance to accountability of grant recipients, or investees, it is not clear what the accountability and transparency requirement on behalf of the venture philanthropists themselves are. The democratic deficit that characterises conventional foundations, and necessitates the role of bodies such as the Charity Commission, becomes even more pronounced in the field of venture philanthropy, particularly as funders may not necessarily wish to operate within the realm of charity law.

Second, other criticisms of venture philanthropy relate to the real knowledge of venture philanthropists. Are venture philanthropists really in a position to assess community needs? Do they really understand what needs to be done and how it can be achieved? There is a saying in Silicon Valley among young entrepreneurs that the best money is smart money—are venture philanthropists able to add significant value to organisations beyond their capital investments? Is it really going to be helpful to have donors with little or no non-profit experience moonlighting for the organisations they fund?

Third, venture philanthropy raises important questions about the role of non-profit organisations and the standards against which they should be judged. Venture philanthropists tend to focus on efficiency and effectiveness and performance, but some non-profits would argue that this fails to take into account the importance of participation and process which are central to the concepts of civil society and social capital building.

Venture philanthropy may speak to issues of efficiency and effectiveness of grant-making but it fails to address the more fundamental questions about the role of foundations and philanthropy in a democratic modern society, the donor's power to select some priorities rather than others, and the actual ability of foundations to focus on the root causes of social problems.[16]

In sum, while we find much of interest and benefit in the venture philanthropy model, we also see several shortcomings.

## Conclusion

The changes outlined above have placed new demands on foundations, increased the complexity of grant-making and investment decisions, and require a radical rethinking of foundations' roles and relationships. These changes place significant demands on volunteer trustees to guide and

---

[16] For a discussion of the varieties of venture philanthropy, and critics, see Carrington, 2002.

control foundations. Organisations such as the National Center for Non-profit Boards in the US and the Trustee Services Unit in England are evidence of growing recognition of the need for attention to governance matters if trustees are to be able to exercise their proper responsibilities in a new and more demanding policy environment. The profusion of codes and standards of governance and accountability is another manifestation of concern. But these initiatives tend to focus on structures and processes.

Similarly, most of the major recent developments in philanthropy in the UK seek to increase the volume of philanthropy by providing new structures and brokering services. For example, the Funding Network provides a vehicle for 'small' givers (£1,000 a year); the Giving Campaign and the Legacy Promotion Campaign target financial advisers; The London Partnership, New Philanthropy Capital, Project Connect, and Sharegift are all forms of brokering services making links among individual funders and between funders and grant seekers.

New structures and processes are important but what the foundation world lacks is a coherent, modern vision that provides legitimacy and direction. 'The worlds of public and private are significantly disjoined. And for the first time in the history of the philanthropic foundation the search for leadership and intelligent management appears to be in a state of crisis' (Karl and Karl 1999: 71).

Foundations are operating in a changed and changing environment which is only slowly being recognised and of which many remain unaware. The changing context and the responses foundations find, or fail, to formulate create both threats and opportunities.

The threats include:

- loss of any coherent, dynamic, defensible philosophy and roles;

- increasing questioning of the effectiveness and efficiency of foundations—getting caught in the dominant performance measurement culture;

- increasing questioning of the value and legitimacy of foundations' privileged legal and fiscal position;

- increasing demands for accountability and transparency;

- increasing risk of having unrealistic roles imposed upon them by others; and

- increasing risk of failure to attract new philanthropists.

Opportunities include: the chance to

- to develop new, more robust roles and rationales for foundations in an assertive way;

- to redefine foundations' relationships with government in a positive and clear approach;

- to rethink foundation governance and relationships in ways which would make foundations more vibrant and effective organisations;

- to resolve some of the fundamental dilemmas of policy and practice which have dogged foundations for decades;

- to make a genuinely distinctive contribution to the public good which plays to foundation strengths and reduces weaknesses; and

- to reinvigorate philanthropic foundation formation for the 21st century.


The challenge for philanthropy is not merely one of money; it is fundamentally not even one of legitimacy. It is a challenge of creativity and a lack of both knowledge and awareness of interdependence. The ability of foundations to meet this challenge could provide the key to reinventing philanthropic foundations, their legitimacy, and their sustained growth. We think that creativity is the central issue for the future of foundations—a proposal to which we turn in the next chapter.

# Chapter 5

# The Creative Foundation

# Introduction

In previous chapters we have argued that foundations need to find new and coherent roles due to changes in the changed and changing environments in which they work. Foundations face new threats, including questions regarding their accountability and legitimacy. They are in danger of having inappropriate roles and relationships thrust upon them, as well as inappropriate performance measures, if they do not seize the significant opportunities open to them and articulate new and more positive roles which play to their strengths rather than their weaknesses. Once they have redefined their potentially significant roles in society, other necessary structural and cultural changes should become easier to identify.

Almost 20 years ago, Pifer (1984a: 14) complained of 'a kind of pervasive arrogance, perhaps almost inevitable in the giving field', that he also saw permeating many foundations. Now, however, in private if not in public, foundations are becoming restless. The old formulae no longer suffice—not least because governments have moved the goal posts and changed the rules of the game, and venture philanthropists appear content without creating formal foundations. Many foundation trustees and staff appear hungry for change.

Some seek comfort in the new menu of venture capital, strategic philanthropy, social investment, and so on, which gives them a new language to describe what they do and perhaps even some new ways of doing things. But the new menu is chewing gum: it has the elasticity to stretch to most things but is devoid of nutritional value. The new menu does not feed foundations' desire for new roles or some deeper rationale and purpose. It does not give them the positive vision and robustness to deal with the threats and opportunities they know confront them. Could it be that venture capital, strategic philanthropy, social investment, and the like are the *cuisine minceur* of philanthropy—sounds good, looks good, but ultimately leaves you feeling empty without any real answers to the crucial questions: what are the roles of foundations in modern democracies, and how can foundations justify their lack of democratic accountability? In essence, we argue that the 'new menu' of philanthropy deals with processes primarily and very little with values and outcomes.

## Starting with an Outcome

To develop its true potential a foundation needs to start with an outcome it wants to achieve (Carrington, 2002). Very broadly, foundations currently pursue two types of outcome:

- The temporary amelioration of 'undesirable circumstances and conditions' for a limited number of people: for example, grants for holidays or outings for disadvantaged children, or grants to purchase equipment for holiday play schemes for these children. In most cases the desired outcome is achieved by the grant per se (charitable gift giving).

- Some type of longer-term change to benefit a larger and unknown number of people. Pursuit of longer-term change may be expressed in grants for medical research, for demonstration projects, and so on. In these cases the desired outcome is not achieved by the grant per se but rather requires wider and longer-term change by a variety of social actors, groups, and institutions not directly involved in the grant-making relationship.

This second type of outcome is much more difficult to achieve but, as we have suggested above, provides the most convincing legitimisation for foundations' lack of democratic governance. This innovative change role turns the fundamental weakness of foundations into a potential virtue.

We argue that endowed foundations need to stop playing to their weaknesses and start playing to their strengths instead. But to be able to do so requires some degree of honesty and 'out-of-the-box' thinking. Most important, foundations have to acknowledge that they have neither the resources nor the democratic mandate to fill gaps, to provide everything the state does not provide, and to support unpopular causes in the long term. What is more, foundations should no longer use resource limitations as an excuse to turn down grant-seekers, but should make it very clear that they are not in the business of stepping in to cover what governments, market firms, or other non-profit organisations might be better at providing.

Foundations should stop pretending they could be more and do more only if they had more resources. In very fundamental ways, endowed foundations need to learn the three R's: *realism* about their resources relative to costs of provision; *rationalism* about the ways in which social change occurs and their limitations in this process; and *recognition* that charity has very limited power in overcoming social disadvantage.

Put differently, lack of both resources, relative to the costs of provision, and democratic mandate are foundations' key weaknesses, but they are also among their key potential strengths. The key is that foundation resources are 'free' relative to government and market.

Foundations enjoy the luxury of freedom from market and political constraints and constituencies. They also enjoy the luxury of perpetuity. Foundations have sufficient resources and 'space' to allow them to think, to be truly innovative, to take risks, to fail, and to take the longer-term view. Furthermore, in an important sense, foundations exist in a world of their own, they do not fully belong to any one sector but have, or could have, a foot in all; they are not, yet, dominated by any one professional group and thus have the freedom and space to think and work across conventional wisdoms, disciplinary, organisational, and sectoral boundaries. These characteristics of endowed foundations give them the potential to make a contribution to society way beyond that which their limited resources might suggest.

Doing more of the same, or tinkering with existing approaches, has, on the whole, not worked. Foundations, fund-raising voluntary organisations and government are still pouring money into old problems, as well as some new ones. Society desperately needs truly new approaches based on creative thinking and working that go beyond existing professional, departmental, and organisational boundaries and mind sets.

Innovation and creativity are central to foundations' claims about themselves and one of the key opportunities for endowed foundations to find a new legitimacy. Focusing on creativity and innovation turns endowed foundations' greatest weakness into their greatest strength and plays to their unique institutional characteristics: their relatively independent resource base and their freedom from market and political pressures. In other words, foundations have the freedom to take a longer-term view in ways and to an extent that is not open to politicians, businesses, and fund-raising voluntary organisations. At the same time, we have to realise that much of what endowed foundations currently do could also be done, and perhaps done at least equally well, by corporate foundations, community and government-initiated foundations, and other voluntary organisations, even public agencies and businesses. Endowed foundations should therefore concentrate on doing those things only they have the potential to do better than other institutions.

Endowed foundations have, in an important sense, had it right all along. The only justification for independence from government and market accountability (as distinct from transparency) is their potential to be a source of innovation and creativity that is unconstrained by short-term market forces and political considerations. But the potentially unique contributions foundations could make to society, that is, their signature characteristics in innovation and creativity, have become inspirational clichés without much of a realistic content in terms of performance and grant-making practice. The visions and roles foundations are casting for themselves must involve the revitalisation of their aspirations, giving them real meaning and verve.

This sounds easy but in reality it means going back to basics, questioning the fundamental frameworks with which the foundation operates. Pursuing innovation and creativity as an outcome means clarifying what we mean by these terms, the process and the circumstances under which they occur.

# What is Innovation?

As stated in Chapter 2, by 'innovation' we understand a special kind of change that rests on a new idea applied to initiating or improving an activity, service, or product. Innovation is the generation, acceptance, and implementation of new ideas, processes, products or services' (Kanter 1983:20). Innovations can involve radical breakthroughs, significant procedural modifications, or minor improvement or 'architectural' changes. Not all innovations are technical in nature. Some are primarily about new ways of 'seeing' issues, conceptualising phenomena, and 'framing' problems. These paradigmatic shifts may occur less frequently than procedural and programmatic innovations, but they tend to lead to some of the most profound changes. It is in these new ways of 'framing' problems, and ways of addressing them, that foundations have a potentially very special role to play.

New ideas not put into practice are not innovations. New ideas, which are put into practice but only on a very small scale, are low-level or sub-innovations. Larger-scale and, crucially, sustainable innovations to achieve real change require dissemination, influence on policy (whether government policy or policy within an organisation), acceptance, replication; ultimately innovations for lasting change need to become embedded in practice. But innovation is a process, not a once-and-for-all task. Circumstances change, new demands arise, new knowledge and understanding emerge, once-new ideas and practices grow old, stale, and less relevant—and the process of innovation has to begin again. Successful innovations typically show a distinctive combination of characteristics (see Kanter 1983):

First, innovation involves a significant degree of *uncertainty* in the sense that both process and outcome may be difficult to predict. This means that foundations should embrace that uncertainty, be open about it, and not hide behind performance and output indicators or 'save' funding practices to justify their legitimacy. Supporting innovation has to take the risk of failure into account. The important point is that foundations, unlike other institutions, can afford to take such risks.

Second, innovations are *knowledge-intensive* as those close to the locus of innovation tend to possess most knowledge about the definition of the situation, the process involved, and the possible outcomes, at least at the initial stage. Foundations should therefore take advantage of knowledge management, involve grants officers more fully in executive decision-making, and seek more diverse board compositions to draw in different experiences and knowledge sets.

Third, innovations are typically *controversial*, as they tend to face established interests and may take resources away from alternative uses. Thus, foundations should not shy away from controversy and the public eye but be open about what they fund and for what reasons. Innovation is not just a matter of new ideas and practices: innovation is a political process as well in the sense that change requires challenging existing accepted policies and practices, whether at the level of government or of organisations.

Fourth, and finally, innovations tend to *reach across established boundaries* in organisations, fields, or sectors. Indeed, foundations are critical boundary-spanners in modern society, and they should avoid becoming niche institutions catering to specific constituencies.

Thus, endowed foundations are uniquely placed to cope with uncertainty and controversy. They have the resources to promote, gather, disseminate, and develop knowledge; and as discussed above they also have the potential to reach across established disciplinary, organisational, and sectoral boundaries. Of course, not everything foundations do, and not every grant they make, has to meet the innovation criteria we just described. What we argue, however, is that foundations should be more innovative because, of all modern institutions, they are the most able to be innovative.

There are two additional aspects of innovation that are worth keeping mentioning explicitly in this context, even though we hinted at them at various points. Both are central results of research on innovation.

First, ever since Coleman's study of innovation in the late 1950's (Coleman, Menzel, and Katz 1957), a persistent finding of innovation research has been that innovation and adaptation of innovative ideas and practices happens at the margins, not at the centre of the system under consideration. The centres of power and wealth in society are rarely the locus of innovation—be it in the field of technology, economic, culture, or politics. More likely, innovations spring from individuals, groups, and organisations outside the mainstream.

This finding holds significant lessons for foundations: to be innovative, one has to remain outside the centre, and should not be part of the 'inner system'. In other words, to encourage innovation and renewal, foundations and their representatives must divest themselves of their political, economic, and cultural elite status, and relocate more to the margins of the country's power structure. At the very least, foundations should draw in fewer of the 'great and good' of society, and look instead toward the border regions where elites and wider society meet.

The second major finding of innovation research is that innovators are encouraged in situations or networks that involve significant overlaps among groups, cultures, and perspectives in 'being able to see the wood for the trees'. Innovations happen not in isolation but at cultural, political, and social crossroads and in situations that bring different and frequently contradictory elements together. For foundations to become innovators, therefore, they must actively seek out dissenting voices and create opportunities for bringing them together. As boundary-spanners, foundations are uniquely qualified to create such forums for innovative ideas and practices to develop. In other words, foundations could be the creative force behind social innovations of all kinds.

## Creating Creativity

Drawing on Landry's work on the creative city, this section considers foundations as creative organisations. According to Landry (2000), creativity requires 'resourcefulness and problem solving capability based on thinking in an open-minded way'. Creativity is a 'frame of mind which questions rather than criticises, which asks "why is this so?" and is not content to accept "it has always been like this"'. Creativity does not challenge only things seen as a problem but also things currently thought of as adequate. 'Creative people and institutions are willing to rewrite procedures or principles and so to imagine future scenarios, conditions, inventions, applications, adaptations and processes. They look for threads among the seemingly disparate, bringing together unthought-of combinations that solve a problem. Most important, perhaps, is the capacity to look at situations in an integrated, holistic way, laterally and flexibility' (Landry 2000: 13). 'Creative people work at the edge of their competency not at the centre of it' (Perkins quoted in Landry 2000: 14).

## Are Foundations Creative Milieux?

Endowed foundations are not, never can be, and never should be substitutes for government and statutory provision. They have neither the resources nor the democratic mandate to take on these roles. Nevertheless, endowed foundations have never been more important than they are today. Most societies are increasingly dominated by short-term market values and competitiveness. Endowed foundations offer the possibility of alternative viewpoints that take a wider and longer-term view. Landry (2000: Ch. 1) identifies seven characteristics of a creative milieu:

- a level of original and deep knowledge coupled with a ready supply of skills, competence, and people who have the need and the capacity to communicate with each other;

- a sound financial basis, adequate room to allow room for experimentation without tight regulation;

- an imbalance between the perceived needs of decision-makers, business people, artists, scientists, and social critics and actual opportunities;

- the capacity to deal with complexity and uncertainty about future changes in cultural, scientific, and technological fields;

- good possibilities for informal and spontaneous communication internally and externally; an environment catering for diversity and variety;

- a multi-disciplinary and dynamically synergistic environment which especially links development in the science and the arts, and

- structural instability.

Foundations clearly have the potential for one of the major qualities of a creative milieu: a sound financial basis, adequate provision to allow room for experimentation without tight regulation, in part derived from their lack of accountability and freedom from the strictures of performance measurement.

But it is much less clear that foundations currently display other qualities of a creative milieu. It is not clear that all foundations possess 'original and deep knowledge', not least because of the way in which trustees and staff are selected and because of foundations' tendency to lack focus. What is more, it is not clear that foundations engage in high levels of diverse internal and external communications, not least because their resource independence and culture of isolationism do not encourage this.

Furthermore, it is also not clear that foundations are multi-disciplinary organisations; and they are unlikely to experience structural instability and thus change. When change, especially in staffing, occurs it does appear to be a trigger for new thinking, but this is rarely built into foundations by, for example, fixed terms of office for trustees and staff.

Creativity requires not just a creative milieu but also the triggers which can kick-start innovative processes. Many of the triggers of creativity in other types of organisations do not apply to endowed, resource-independent foundations. Crucially, the pressures of necessity and scarcity, inescapable for many organisations, are pretty much escapable for foundations. As self-defining and self-financing organisations, foundations do not face the same sort of pressures. As resource-independent organisations existing in perpetuity, foundations are also immune to obsolescence, further compounded by the fact that their 'customers' (grant applicants) are very unlikely to tell them that their purposes are obsolescent.

Similarly, creative triggers of ambition, aspiration, and competition do not apply to foundations in any obvious way. Foundations rarely compete with each other (except perhaps in size of assets), and without competition the motives of ambition and aspiration are less pressing. Again, political change, criticism, crisis, and structural instability—important triggers for creativity in other organisations—are 'ills' foundations rarely suffer. Interestingly, however, when foundations do experience either significant reduction or increase in income, this sometimes provides a trigger for creative thinking about programmes. Examples in Britain include the Baring Foundation and Esmee Fairbairn Foundation.

Other triggers of creativity, such as discovery, luck, participation, ideas gathering, and learning from others, are not fully exploited by many foundations because learning and networking are not part of their culture. Similarly, foundations rarely seem to create triggers for creativity such as implementing creativity policies and symbolic acts like prizes, competitions, landmark events, and branded concepts.

Foundations could, however, do more to engineer triggers for creativity by, for example, placing a higher priority on learning internally and externally, spending more time talking and listening, increasing rates of leadership change by appointing staff and trustees for fixed terms (as in BBC Children in Need and Carnegie UK Trust), and developing policies and processes positively to reward creativity. Effective ways of encouraging and rewarding creativity require discussion and research, including reviews of work in the for-profit sector on these topics.

## Grant-making Practices and Support for Creativity and Innovation

As discussed above, foundations have traditionally seen themselves as supporters of creativity and innovation. In the previous section we suggested that foundations do indeed have great potential as creative milieux but lack some of the usual triggers for developing internal creative capacity to inform policies, priorities, and grant-making.

In this section we argue that conventional grant-making practices also do little to support creativity and lasting innovation by grant recipients. We suggest that the process of grant giving neither recognises nor encourages conditions for creativity or innovation. In grant-making, there is little room for change, luck, or the unexpected. Foundations work with inadequate theories of the triggers and authors of creativity and conditions for successful implementation and effective innovation; they also work with largely unarticulated and implausible approaches to social change.

Sociologists have long argued that individuals and organisations make sense of the world and what they do by means of various frameworks and 'theories in use'. These frameworks are taken for granted and rarely made explicit and critically examined (Bolman and Deal 1991; Powell and DiMaggio 1991). They are common-sense, routine-based frameworks that frequently operate in the background of why and how things are done. If we work back from foundation grant-making practices, what frameworks and 'theories' do foundations appear to operate with? Foundations' 'theories in use' can be analysed under four main headings: the roles of voluntary organisations, relations with the state and government, the role of money, and conditions for 'success' and social change.

## Roles of Voluntary Organisations

Most foundations appear to operate on the assumption that (i) what voluntary organisations choose to do is an adequate index of social needs and problems of society, and (ii) voluntary organisations are the major locus of new thinking and innovation generally. These assumptions persist despite numerous studies that demonstrate that the existence of voluntary organisations is very imperfectly related to social need (see Anheier and Kendall 2001; Flynn and Hodgkinson 2002; Perrow 2001), and that voluntary organisations are not, despite their rhetoric, particularly innovative (Kramer 1990).

# Relations with Government

The absence of government from most foundations' implicit theories of innovation may stem from some deep-seated assumptions regarding government and their relations with it. Unfortunately, in the UK we have no studies of foundation leaders' political beliefs and values along the lines of that by Nagai, Lerner, and Rothman (1994) in the US. The impression, however, is that most UK foundation representatives strongly believe that independence from the state is vitally important and that working with government is viewed with suspicion, if not avoided altogether. Although many foundations act as though they believe that 'big' government is bad, they have also traditionally assumed that what foundations start, government will, and should, continue (see, for example, Douglas and Wildavsky 1980/1; Karl and Karl 1999). At one level, foundations see themselves almost as equal partners with government; at another, they stress their independence. As a result, the relationship between government and foundations is frequently highly ambiguous.

# The Role of Money

Similarly, the assumptions foundations make regarding the power of money are complex, if not contradictory. Grant-making—the transfer of financial resources from the foundation to other organisations—implicitly assumes that social problems can be solved directly or indirectly by money. Money is the root of all solutions, and more money to make more grants makes foundations more effective. The assumption is that we know, or could know, what needs to be done; money is all that is missing. Furthermore, it is assumed that it is important to avoid having no disposable income (silting up) by committing grants long-term.

But at the same time many foundations' grant-making practices tend to operate on the assumption that for grant recipients too much money is damaging and regular money for core funding is bad in that it creates dependence. Money is also 'bad' for those in greatest need. Money is the solution to the problems of voluntary organisations but not, it seems, to those of users. In addition, it is often assumed, wrongly, that giving a small amount of money will provide the legitimacy to lever more resources elsewhere. Money, it is assumed, breeds more money.

## Success and Social Change

Foundation grant-making practices rest on a complex set of implicit theories that have to do with 'success', sustainability, and social change. Most obviously these theories include the assumption that 'good and successful' projects are a function of good ideas, well-thought through plans, and good organisation; it takes a year (or maybe three) for a project to prove itself; 'good and proven' projects will find more funding when the foundation grant ends; and social change comes from the bottom up. More fundamentally, current dominant approaches to grant-making assume that it is possible to predict and create a knowable future (Fowler 1995). Problems have causes that are singular, knowable, and uncontested; there is a known solution and money can produce this solution.

The processes of grant making and in particular of grant assessment are based on a number of questionable assumptions. Among them are:

- Good organisations have within themselves the capacity to achieve what they set out to achieve.

- Organisational structures and processes, management, and financial resources are major determinants and predictors of organisational capacity and achievements.

- Evidence of clear objectives, planning, and control processes are particularly important indicators of the 'good' or capable organisation.

- Sustainability and future funding is something for which the 'good' organisation can plan and has planned.

- The future of voluntary organisations and the environments in which they work will be a continuation of present trends' (Leat 1999).

These are just some of the assumptions underlying the rational model of planning and change implicitly adopted by many foundations and expressed in grant-making processes. Typical grant-making processes assume that a plan can be made in advance; success requires that the plan is adhered to; the organisation and its plan exist in a hermetically sealed compartment in which external factors do not matter or, equally implausible, are both foreseeable and controllable. A more realistic view might be that:

- Organisations exist in contexts made up of, among other factors, other organisations whose actions wittingly and unwittingly impinge on, constrain, subvert, and support each other.

- Knowledge, communication, coordination, and compliance are imperfect.

- Resources are limited.

- Social conditions, organisations, and individuals do not stand still.

- Workable social plans are usually those that provide a basis for departure rather than a blueprint for action.

- Risks are ever present and certainty is in short supply.

- Linkages and networks with other voluntary, statutory, and private organisations often underlie successful interventions.

- People—individuals—may matter more than structures, not least in their capacity to constantly adapt to new demands and obstacles and to make relationships (Hogwood and Gunn 1984; Leat 1999).

## New Roles for Foundations

There is a growing realisation that money alone is not sufficient to address many of the most intractable problems of modern society. Conventional ways no longer work, not least because problems increasingly cut across organisational and professional boundaries. Lack of knowledge and inadequate theories of social change, effects of narrow organisational and professional perspectives, and short-term thinking limit our menu of solutions.

There are endless sound-bite solutions and entrenched clichés and positions sometimes based on sectoral, professional, or organisational pride and advantage. But genuinely creative, innovative ideas are in short supply. Endowed foundations, free of market and political constraints and considerations, and as yet uncaptured by one professional or disciplinary group, have the potential to fill this gap in real creativity and innovation. Foundations can, if they choose, think the unthinkable, ignoring disciplinary and professional boundaries. They can take risks, consider approaches others say can't possibly work—and they can fail with no terminal consequences. Equally important, foundations have the luxury of being able to take a longer-term view. Foundations are free to be imaginative and creative, working across sectoral, organisational, professional, and disciplinary boundaries, without the sometimes stifling constraints of short-term, ill-conceived performance measurement criteria.

But this is not an easy option. It is not 'business as usual'. If foundations are to be genuinely creative and innovative they will need to put aside preconceptions and existing theories in use. They will need to accept that the voluntary sector does not have a monopoly on creativity and innovation; they will need to look for good ideas, creative people, and groups in all sectors. They will need to accept that creativity and innovation may happen quickly, more slowly, or not at all. They will need to accept that creativity and innovation come in various places, at various times, by various means.

Positively pursuing creativity and innovation will require changes in foundation structures and processes. Foundations will need to audit their structures, practices, and processes against Landry's (2000) list of preconditions for creativity.

# Building a Creative Foundation: Preconditions for Creativity

## Personal qualities

According to Landry (2000), both the 'ideas stage' and implementation are creative processes, each requiring a mix of imaginative qualities, people working together across organisations to develop synergies and mutual support. Both stages also require the ability to think openly and flexibly, willingness to take risks, a commitment to constant learning, and the ability to prioritise effectively to avoid routine demands smothering time for innovation.

These points have a number of implications for foundations. Foundations need to work on both 'stages' in the creative process, focusing on ideas generation and following through on implementation. Foundations need to ensure a mix of imaginative qualities among trustees and staff and to make imagination an important recruitment criterion. Foundations need to consider carefully their use of staff and advisers from specialist professional areas and to avoid those who are locked into professional and disciplinary boxes even though such specialist knowledge may have an important role later on; the old polymath advisers often used by earlier foundations may have been more creative. Trustees and staff need to learn how to protect themselves from routine demands and to spend time considering new approaches, at the top of the agenda rather than at the bottom. Trustees and staff need to spend more time, not less, talking to each other and to a wide range of others outside the organisation, across sectors, disciplines, and professions. Crucially, they need to develop cultures and processes for constant learning within and from beyond the foundation (Carrington, 2002).

## Will and leadership

Creativity and innovation require will and leadership—but less in the sense of exercising power than in giving vision and meaning. They require energy and dynamism, discipline and control, concentration and focus, resolve and readiness to take decisions, patience, perseverance and tolerance, initiative and courage, and the capacity to organise, integrate, and synthesise. Foundations need to consider ways in which they can develop these qualities among staff and trustees, and the changes in culture they may need to institute in order to do so.

Landry (2000) distinguishes between 'ordinary, innovative and visionary' leaders. Ordinary leaders reflect the desires or needs of the group they lead. Innovative leaders ask questions to draw out latent needs, bringing fresh insights to new areas. Visionary leaders harness the power of completely new ideas. The traditional approach of foundations has been, at best, to be ordinary leaders, responding to the demands of voluntary sector applicants who are often mired in narrow, single-issue approaches to ongoing social problems. If foundations wish to become innovative, or even visionary, leaders they need to be prospecting proactively for truly new ideas and approaches from any source they can find. Innovative and visionary leaders understand the power of stories of what new ideas could achieve and how to get there. Foundations need to become storytellers of change outcomes promoting their stories far and wide. This might have the added bonus of encouraging the new, young rich to invest in the exciting business of developing creative, 'out-of-the-box' approaches to intractable social issues.

## Human diversity and access to varied talent

Real creativity and innovation require new approaches, new combinations, a mix of perspectives, cultures, and disciplines. They need outsiders to give freshness and all the virtues that go with lack of insider knowledge and first impressions. They need insiders to provide deep knowledge and understanding.

If foundations are to be creative and innovative in their own thinking and in their grant-making, they need to find ways of ensuring access to diverse, varied talents and ideas. They need to be able to combine access to deep knowledge and understanding with access to those who can see things in a fresh light unencumbered by preconceptions from the past. Core staff may be the source of deep knowledge; trustees and external advisers might be recruited to provide new perspectives, or vice versa.

For example, instead of selecting trustees for their expertise in the foundation's area of interest, a foundation might decide to seek out trustees with skills and knowledge from a very different area and discipline. One role of these trustees might be to play the part of two-year olds constantly asking 'why?—'why is this a good idea?', 'why is this likely to add value?', 'why is this seen as a solution to that problem?'— and to reject answers along the lines of 'because that's how its done'. In the process of answering these 'two-year-old trustees', the foundation will be forced to make explicit its assumptions, some of which may not withstand scrutiny in the light of day.

## Organisational culture

Creativity and innovation require particular organisational cultures. The culture needs to positively encourage 'deviant' thinking and working, and expanding possibilities, 'pushing the envelope' in the current jargon, and learning within and from outside the organisation. Creative organisations understand the virtues of failure—but they also understand that there is no virtue in failure unless it is analysed and lessons learned. Cultures of creativity recognise the value of catalysts but, because innovation is risky and scary, acknowledge that catalysts need rewards and incentives to become involved.

If foundations are to be truly creative organisations, their cultures need to meet these conditions. Foundation cultures need to encourage 'deviants' rather than 'yes' people embedded in conventional professional thinking and working. They need to place a high value on talking and thinking, brainstorming and lateral thinking inside the organisation and with the widest range of other people and organisations. They need to audit the knowledge to which they have, or could have, access, placing as much value on the knowledge and ideas of grants-officers and assessors as they do on that of trustees, senior staff, and 'experts'.

They need to do more than talk about risks and failure, setting out systematically to analyse and learn from failures and successes. Instead of treating evaluation and analysis of current and past grants as an expensive luxury, foundation cultures need to define these as necessities. Instead of worrying about spending too much on learning and evaluation, foundation cultures need to encourage anxiety about the costs of spending too little. Talking about valuing creativity and innovation is not enough; foundations may sometimes need to back talk with events, prizes, and competitions which will underline their commitment and bring new ideas, ways of working, and creative people to their attention.

## Organisational capacity

As Landry emphasises, good intentions are not enough to make a creative, innovative organisation. Creative organisations need organisational capacities to make creativity work. They need leadership capacity, technical competence, and up-to-date knowledge about what is going on. They need the capacity to identify strategic issues and priorities and to take a longer-term view. They need the capacity to spend time listening to and consulting others. They need to command loyalty and trust. They need to be able to enthuse other decision-makers and create consensus via a shared vision. They need to have the ability and the time to form partnerships and to work within them. And they need to have the strength to make difficult decisions.

Foundations are well placed to develop these capacities but they will need changes in culture and practice, time and commitment, and new skills. Crucially, foundations will need to learn to take a longer-term view and to accept that, working alone, they can achieve very little. Working with others, within and across sectors, will require new values, new processes, and new skills. The Bridge House Estates Trust Fund work with Mayoral candidates in London and its funding of London Sustainability Exchange, and City Parochial Foundation's work on school exclusion, are two examples of foundations recognising the need to work across sectors.

## Networking and associative structures

Networking feeds effective creativity and innovation. Wide, deep, and dense networks increase the capacity for ideas and learning not merely because they increase access to existing approaches but also because they increase the likelihood of generating new ideas. Networks are essential to creative effective implementation; in real life very few social issues come in boxes with a single label or owner.

Again, foundations need to spend time looking outwards, listening and learning. Some foundations already do this to a degree. For example, Barnwood House Trust receives briefings from the local authority and health authority, thus increasing its knowledge of issues and who is doing what; Lloyds TSB Foundation for England and Wales has a special budget for supporting collaboration across sectors, stimulating transfer of knowledge and ideas to make a real impact.

But foundations need to make networking part of the everyday activity, rather than special programmes or events. They need to increase the permeability of their organisational boundaries, to develop antennae finely tuned to creative ideas, to become, in the jargon, network organisations. The Association of Charitable Foundations has made an important start in encouraging foundations to talk to each other. If foundations are to become truly creative, innovative organisations, they need networks that extend across organisations, sectors, and countries. They need wide, deep, and dense local networks for local initiatives and implementation, but they also need networks at regional and national levels. Even if they do not give grants or work internationally, they need international networks to stimulate new questions, ideas, and solutions.

They need to spend more time, not less, meeting and talking to others, and more time outside rather than inside the organisation.

## Facets of the Creative Foundation

Endowed foundations have the space and resources to stand back and question the mantras of the day and to encourage truly creative thinking to address the issues into which they, and others, have invested resources, financial and otherwise, in the hope of creating lasting effects. What they need to do is to occupy that space to a much greater extent than is presently the case.

In this sense, the creative foundation is not simply a foundation that stresses, encourages and funds innovation. Creativity as the signature element of the foundation of the future is principally about a way of working. It is as much about the approach and the process as it is about the outcome.

Clearly, much effort has to flow into the development of a model for the creative foundation. A range of possible legal implications and frameworks has to be considered, in particular in the light of the recent report by the Cabinet Office (2002), suggesting new legal forms for charitable organisation. The oganisational and governance structure and mode of operation of creative foundations has to be worked out, with special emphasis on 'network elements', information and knowledge management, communication flows, and a mix of operative approaches.

The best way to approach this task is to engage in a systematic search for innovation and creativity in existing foundations, and to draw in the lessons from new forms and developments in the field, in particular venture philanthropy and strategic philanthropy. For us, this will be the next step, and a necessary one for developing the notion of the creative foundation from its current idea stage to something more concrete and practical.

Against the background of this assessment of innovation and creativity in the world of philanthropy, the future challenge will be to design structures and processes that transcend existing boundaries in exploring new ways of thinking in identifying and addressing issues. The task is to develop a system—or philanthropic organisation—that feeds on new thoughts, and not money alone, and that if necessary re-conceptualises problems and issues, makes new connections, and tries new methods and approaches.

This will require intellectual guidance and solid grounding in an understanding of the proper role of foundations in society—their particular role in addressing and solving social problems of all kinds, and their special way of contributing to solutions and new methods of intervention. In other words, the creative foundation, like the philanthropic innovators a century ago, needs to work its way through a theory of social change to position itself in relation to other actors as well as the set of issues it wants to address.

The creative foundation will not necessarily be a grant-making foundation. New combinations of how foundations achieve their goals are called for. This may involve special projects run by the foundation in co-operation with others, operating own programmes, funding networks, and venture philanthropy type approaches, in addition to more conventional grant-making.

Whatever its way of operating, the creative foundation is outward looking, and draws on a range of knowledge and expertise from the highly respected to the often neglected expertise of those at the front line, whether as funders, experts, workers or users. The creative foundation is prepared, if necessary, to act on a number of levels from the 'grass roots' to the global (e.g. the World Bank, European Union), and is opportunistic in seeking partners, putting emphasis on networks rather than 'go it alone' approaches.

Finally, the creative foundation knows that good ideas do not disseminate themselves and is prepared to spend time and money on dissemination and marketing. It is above all a learning organisation, treating its knowledge resources at all levels of the organisation with the same care it devotes to the management of its financial assets.

We are not arguing that all foundations should become creative foundations over night, leaving behind what they did in the past. Numerous existing foundations carry out excellent programmes and achieve important, sometimes admirable, outcomes. Yet for the many that do not, and for those that seek better and forward-looking visions and roles, the creative foundation as suggested here might be a way forward. At the minimum, what we would like to see is that more foundations think about their role in modern society in the context of what we regard as their true *raison d'être*: the innovative pursuit of public benefit.

# Chapter 6

# Towards a New Agenda

The main argument we put forth in this report was that the institution of an endowed, philanthropic foundation is clearly a good and potentially important element of modern societies. Foundations fit in well with the way advanced democratic societies are developing, in particular the nexus between private and public responsibilities and benefit in an era of 'small' government and greater social diversity. However, the second part of our argument is that current visions, roles, and, above all, forms of foundations make it difficult for them to fulfil the promise they hold. Against this backdrop, and to develop a new vision and legitimate role, we made a case for innovation as the signature characteristic of the modern foundation.

Foundations are little-known or examined warehouses of wealth. Foundations do not have customers or constituents to please. Because they have permanent, independent income they can please themselves, making decisions about what to support, and where, in private and without reference to democratic priorities. Free from these constraints, foundations can help shape new agendas, create new centres of power and influence, and thereby affect social change in the broadest sense. This is the great potential they hold, but is also the aspect we found most wanting.

We argued that the organisational form of foundations makes it in fact difficult to remain innovative, and suggested that it is easier for foundations to become conventional funding bodies set in their ways than to remain the flexible, change-oriented, and innovative organisations to which they may have originally aspired. That foundations are not typically the centres of innovation they claim to be is not surprising given the way in which they are governed and managed.

Too many foundations' trustees are self-perpetuating oligarchies, drawn in large measure from among 'the great and the good'. Too many foundation staff seem to stay in the same post for considerable periods of time, with little upward and lateral career movement. Foundation cultures stress the need to avoid spending money on research, thinking, and discussion, especially outside the organisation. Charity law requires that foundations remain true to the original donor's wishes irrespective of their relevance to needs, unless and until the situation becomes untenable. In short, foundations are built for stability not change, even though a broader interpretation of *cy près* may offer more flexibility in the future.

Instead of focusing on the underlying weakness of foundations, calls among politicians and foundation representatives for greater philanthropy in society typically focus on more money. Yet the real challenge in philanthropy is a not one of more monetary resources but of knowledge and creativity. Foundations claim to be sources of innovation in society but in reality their overall spending patterns suggest that they support well-recognised causes. They become niche funders, addressing particular problems for specific groups of recipients with predictable, stable patterns of disbursement, or perhaps following the fashion of the moment. Yet, to be and remain innovative over time, foundations have to be more outward-looking and somewhat footloose organisations that migrate to new fields and topics if the competitive advantage of other institutions such as business, non-profit service providers, or government agencies surpasses their own.

Foundations' lack of any coherent, robust, modern statement of their role leaves them open to having roles thrust upon them by government. Foundations do not have the resources to substitute for public service provision. At a time when it is increasingly difficult to distinguish between public, voluntary, and business sector values, practices, and thinking, independent foundations have an enormously important role to play in providing a critical creative voice in policy-making and practice. Foundations alone have the capacity to provide a truly independent, alternative voice not yet dominated by any one professional group and beholden to neither market nor state.

In playing this role, foundations' weaknesses—their lack of accountability and lack of professional capture—become their greatest strengths. Foundations need to become more transparent but maintain their independence to question the conventional wisdoms and dominant professional and policy shibboleths of the day.

We followed Kanter (1983) in suggesting that successful innovations typically show a distinctive set of characteristics: uncertainty, knowledge-intensity, controversy, and reaching across established boundaries. We then linked approaches to innovation to notions of creativity, and used Landry's (2000) work on cities as a platform to develop the framework of what we call the 'creative foundation'. We see the creative foundation as a self-confident institution that is not afraid to take risks, that has strong intellectual leadership, and that operates on the basis of sound knowledge management; an institution that is entrepreneurial in its outlook as well as responsible and respectful, and, above all, that embraces the diversity of modern society in finding solutions.

This is the type of foundation that should take the next evolutionary step in the continuing development of philanthropy: from the charitable foundation of the 19th century to the philanthropic foundation of the 20th century, to the creative foundation of the 21st century. Creative foundations are interstitial institutions, located at the crossroads of society rather than in its centre; they are the idea factories that bring about and facilitate innovation in the broadest sense. They add critically to the capacity of modern societies to find solutions to problems of all kinds. In a sense, the creative foundation is a private problem-solving institution for public problems.

It is not necessary for the creative foundation to command massive resources. Indeed, it may well be easier to be creative with small than with large amounts of money. The image of David and Goliath comes to mind, and, in fact, one could make the case that a large number of small and medium-sized foundations would be better for the problem-solving capacity of modern societies than a smaller number of very large foundations. Smallness has the added advantage that problems associated with greater size—for example, bureaucracy, inertia, power— are more easily avoided. What is more, we could expect the creative foundation to make greater use of networking, forging alliances, and pooling resources than larger, conventional funders typically do.

There are a number of potential new roles for foundations in the 21st century. First and foremost, foundations could play a greater role in policy-making generally. Foundations could take greater advantage of their independence to address and referee the difficult issues in identifying the terms on which there can be partnerships of mutual benefit between government, the corporate sector, and the voluntary sector. Foundations could play an important, independent role in promoting debate about a new understanding of the collective good, among many other topics.

Of course, the creative foundation will not come about overnight, and a sustained and systematic effort will be needed to develop more fully the ideas presented here, and to chart the legal and political implications at the macro level and the economic and organisational implications at the micro level. Towards this end, we suggest the following open agenda in the hope that others will add to it. We group these agenda items under the three headings of *Knowledge*, *Basics*, and *Correctives*, and propose a set of more immediate target steps in conclusion.

## Knowledge

The creative foundation requires knowledge about the field in which it works, about the problems and needs it wants to address and how, and, importantly, about itself. Some of the critical agenda items are:

- *Research*. Without better and more research on foundations generally, efforts to develop a platform for the creative foundation will be severely handicapped.

- *Information*. More comprehensive and up-to-date information is needed on foundations generally, and on assets, disbursements, activities funded, organisational structure, and boards specifically. This also includes better needs assessments and a greater understanding of the 'demand side' of foundation activities.

- *Knowledge management*. New ways and means have to be found to make sure that foundations are in a position to acquire and use knowledge effectively and creatively. Importantly, how can foundations become learning organisations that share knowledge and understanding of issues with others?

- *Establish a discussion forum on the future of foundations.* This

  forum would allow a broad debate about the future of foundations, and enlist the ideas and support of experts as well as outsiders from diverse backgrounds.

- *Create a task force.* A task force or working group would be needed to develop the idea of the creative foundation more fully, to look for examples in a systematic way and mine them for insights and so on.

## Basics

This is, of course, the most challenging part of the process towards the development of a creative foundation. A more comprehensive list will undoubtedly emerge as the work goes forward, and we will flag only some of the agenda items we regard as most critical here, and formulate them in the form of questions.

- What kind of deed would the creative foundations require? Can we think of 'creative deeds' that allow for both change and continuity? What will be the role of the Charity Commission in encouraging and monitoring creative deeds? How will this relate to the concept of 'imprestment', which under current law irrevocably ties funds to the charitable purpose once selected?

- What external incentive structures are needed for the creative foundation? Are changes required in the current tax treatment of foundations? Should the creative foundation be located within or outside the boundaries of charity law?

- What internal incentives structures are best for encouraging creativity and innovation in foundations? What roles can grant managers and programme officers play in that regard?

- What is the appropriate governance structure for the creative foundations? Will the near-omnipotent role of boards and the near-complete lack of voice of others have to be rethought?

- Are creative foundations best established with greater flexibility in terms of time? What are the advantages and disadvantages of foundation models that move away from the notion of perpetuity? There is a need to rethink exit options for funders and foundations, and to explore other time-limited models such as project funds.

- Should the creative foundation establish itself as a separate entity, set apart from conventional foundations? The 20th century foundation differentiated itself from 19th century charities? What would be the 21st century equivalent?

## Correctives

Even though models for the creative foundation will take time for development, discussion, and testing, there are nonetheless steps policy-makers and the foundation community can take at present. As before, we will list them only on the understanding that a more complete catalogue of 'things to do' will be drawn up in the future:

- diversify board composition and invite trustees to join for specific time periods only;

- move away from an emphasis of funding organisations and consider funding individuals;

- put less emphasis on performance and impact measurement; instead 'front-load' the grant-making process and take risks;

- concentrate on fuller assessments of grant impact that stress learning over control;

- reverse the trend toward matching funding requirements and challenge grants schemes;

- consider organising and conducting own projects;

- make early discussion of exit options part of foundation grant-making to avoid both funding dependencies and severe disruptions once funding runs out; and

- strengthen the infrastructure for foundations locally, nationally, and internationally in terms of umbrella organisations and lobbying groups.

Thus, to become creative organisations foundations would need to inject change, openness, and flexibility into their structures and practices. As a start, trustees and staff might be appointed on fixed-term contracts, the composition of trustee bodies should be widened, and foundations need to spend time developing wider networks in the real world. They need to develop structures and processes to encourage debate and dissemination of ideas that cross professional boundaries. Taking on the role of creative organisations for the public good could be the flame that ignites the passion and unlocks the wealth of potential philanthropists among younger cohorts.

# Immediate Challenges

In conclusion, we suggest four immediate challenges that have to be approached if the agenda proposed here is to move forward. The first two challenges are specifically addressed to foundation representatives and philanthropists, while the latter two call upon policy-makers primarily.

## Challenge 1: promote a culture of innovation and creativity

- Review induction and training procedures for trustees and foundation staff in terms of innovative thinking.

- Identify exemplary cases of innovation and creativity and best practices; show where innovation and creativity made a difference.

- Establish new forums to identify and put into practice ways of encouraging innovation in the foundation world and rewarding creative grant-making.

## Challenge 2: strengthen diffusion of knowledge and encourage learning

- Develop and establish governance models that treat innovation as process, not as some end product that can be measured with conventional performance indicators.

- Provide incentives for information-sharing about innovative and creative grant-making among foundation staff.

- Support co-operative ventures among foundations, and 'cluster approaches' to creative problem-solving.

- Review the role of umbrella organisations for grant-making foundations.

## Challenge 3: place innovation capacity at the centre of regulatory reforms

- Review the adequacy of current legal frameworks for foundations, in particular the notions of charity, public benefit, imprestment of deed, and trusteeship

- Review the role of the Charity Commission, and the need for a separate supervisory body for grant-making institutions

- Review the impact of globalisation and European Union policy-making on UK philanthropy, and the implications for the current legal framework for foundations.

## Challenge 4: increase the number of medium-sized to large foundations, and encourage new forms of philanthropic institutions, in particular for smaller endowments.

- Target potential founders of small and medium-sized foundations and encourage them to set up innovative, creative institutions outside the conventional frame of organised, charitable foundations.

- Encourage foundations to experiment with new forms, board structures, and grantee relationships.

- Put in place procedures and incentive systems that encourage established foundations to reorganise and transform themselves into more innovative institutions.

Yet, as we embark on the process of developing new visions, roles, and models for foundations, it is important to be open and admit that perhaps too many foundations have lost their way. Old roles and philosophies, if they ever were viable, provide little direction in today's environment. The crisis of confidence in the foundation world is not due to a lack of resources. Indeed, within reasonable expectations, no amount of money and no massive influx of new foundations will solve the fundamental problem philanthropy faces as we enter the 21st century.

As we argued, the roots of the crisis lie in a lack of any clear articulation of coherent vision for foundations, and a lack of sustainable roles that play to their strengths rather than to their weaknesses. Foundations are neither pale nor poor imitations of government, nor are they the chosen tools for venture philanthropists in search of quick fixes. Foundations are something far more important:

*They are the potential powerhouses of creative thinking modern societies need for long-term public benefit.*

We hope that a new debate will now begin to fully explore this potential.

# Appendix 1

Becoming a creative foundation will require cultural and structural change in many foundations. The following 'rules for discouraging creativity and innovation' may, we suggest, enable foundations to identify both the ways in which they currently inadvertently discourage creativity and, by implication, the necessary changes to encourage creativity and innovation.

## Rules for Discouraging Creativity and Innovation

- Ensure that all decisions are made by those likely to have least direct knowledge of what is already being done, what's working, and where real creativity is needed.

- Try to avoid too much knowledge or make sure that it is in a narrow professional area.

- Ensure that there is minimum possible turnover among trustees and staff: these should be jobs for life.

- Institute procedures to ensure that decisions can be made only at set intervals a few times a year.

- Talk to as few people as possible outside the organisation, and do not encourage internal communication by, for example, holding meetings between trustees, staff, and grants officers unless these are semi-social occasions when there is little danger of anything more than polite small talk.

- Spend as little time and resources as possible on meeting and talking with others and finding out what goes on elsewhere. Remember that careless talk can lead to creativity (and anyway they're only interested in your money).

- Do not actively search out ideas and creative people. Wait for them to find you, preferably from established organisations. Actively discourage unsolicited contact.

- Practice NIMBYism—and keep your back yard small.

- Accept only ideas or applications from the voluntary sector.

- Avoid contact with people who do not have some sort of single interest or attachment

- View any organisation without a sound constitution and a well-constructed set of accounts with the deepest suspicion.

- Reward 'spin' rather than ideas. Look out for applications that say the right things in the right language; don't worry if they don't make sense.

- Try not to give any applicant enough money to provide time and space from fund-raising. This should ensure that they are too busy with the means to get over-involved in the end.

- Avoid giving grants to projects that cannot find funding from other foundations.

- Require applicants to provide a plan and budget in advance—and make sure they stick to it even if everything else around them is changing. Remember that flexibility can be dangerously creative.

- The length of grant should be decided by standardised rules rather than the nature of the task.

- Try to ensure that all grants are for as short a time as possible, and institute strict rules forbidding extensions and repeat grants. If a project looks like it may achieve something do not give a further grant: if it's that good someone else will fund it.

- Make it clear to grant recipients that they will be made accountable. Accountability should be seen as an important policing mechanism and not as an opportunity for mutual learning. What matters is that the report is presented—you do not need to bother to read it.

- Make it clear to organisations that you are interested only in success; there is no need to reward success and definitely do not acknowledge, reward, or learn from failure.

- Discourage all forms of reflection and learning and do not allocate time or resources for these activities. Always focus on the next grant; do not waste time looking back.

- If you must practise evaluation make sure that it is restricted to counting things.

- If you do learn something do not waste time and money telling anyone else.

# Appendix 2

Pifer's (1984a: 23) measures of foundation effectiveness, formulated almost 20 years ago, bear repeating today:

Measures of Effectiveness for ALL FOUNDATIONS

- Does the foundation make grants that simply relieve other funders of responsibility?
- Does it aid causes/institutions that benefit only a small/elite group with no need of help?
- Does it make grants for projects so poorly designed as to have no chance of success?
- Does it actively seek out opportunities to spend funds in imaginative and constructive ways?

Measures of Effectiveness for LARGER FOUNDATIONS:

- Does the foundation stand publicly for positive values in society?
- Does it try to play a leadership role in some sphere?
- Is it an effective source for social betterment?
- Is it imaginative in the way it uses resources?
- Is it a centre for the generation of important new ideas?
- Does its value as an institution clearly transcend its value simply as a source of funds?

# Appendix 3

## Excerpts of comments on Innovation and Creativity received by Perri 6

Innovation depends on making analogies, juxtapositions, ideas from other fields, industries, sectors: maybe you should look at the literature on those social structures and cultures that most effectively combine analogical thinking with individualism (obviously many hierarchical cultures sustain high levels of rather static analogical thinking). Disciplines of innovation involve procedures for cultivating analogical thinking, making juxtapositions, borrowing ideas across industries, countries. These can be taught to some extent, but what really sustains them in use is a certain kind of social structure, certain incentives, certain institutions: cognition follows, and doesn't precede organisation.

Why should a creative foundation fund mainly voluntary organisations at all? Why not award money mainly to businesses? After all, they're often more innovative – at least in product innovation. Moreover, most voluntary organisation innovation is the extension of existing products to new clienteles. And your argument is that priority should probably be product innovation. Incidentally, maybe it would help to make more explicit the distinction between product, process and organisational innovation? And why not more awards to government bodies? Despite the blandishments of public choice theory, there is empirical evidence that innovation in the public sector can run at significant levels.

*Institutions for supporting innovation*: Innovation is a discipline. It needs infrastructure. To appreciate the issues of designing institutional infrastructure to support innovation. You might look at the literature on national styles in innovation policy. The basic conclusion of that research was that the organisational infrastructure for supporting innovation had to be congruent with the prevailing social structure and culture of the labour market and the business world. Thus, the Japanese pre-1990 strategies of long term coordination and support from MITI with coordination in R&D at pre-competitive stage worked in the context of the Japanese big business keiretsu structure and culture, but when tried elsewhere, they didn't (with the partial exception of France, which had a similarly *étatiste* social structure and partly similarly oligopolistic ordering of business in "*les trente glorieuses*". Maybe you could raise the issue of institutional infrastructure for syndicated funding by foundations. After all, much of the most innovative work supported by venture capitalists is supported on the basis of syndicated finance.

*Structured knowledge bases as infrastructure for innovation:* People innovate within paradigms. There has to be a knowledge base from which to develop innovation, e.g. new techniques of genetic engineering depend heavily on (a) the existence and availability of a structure knowledge base of the genomes of humans and animals (b) the existence and collaborative character of a community of scientists and researchers, even extending to collaboration at pre-competitive stage in the biotechnology industry. The knowledge base has to be subject to very specific property rights in order to serve this function: people have to be able to draw upon it cheaply, but they also have to be given incentives steadily and continuously to contribute to it. What is the equivalent knowledge base and equivalent set of institutional arrangements for the governance of such a knowledge base and for the design of incentives for, say, personal social services or community development or crime prevention or health promotion? Maybe your report should be more about the ways in which foundations might work together to create such an institutional and cognitive infrastructure for a creative industry of foundations, than about the *individually* creative foundation?

*Industry*: Although some innovations are radical enough to create new industries, most innovations work within existing industries. Bach's and Beethoven's radicalism revolutionised music, but didn't revolutionise the basic division of products and labour that constituted the arts. The new genetic engineering techniques revolutionised what went on in medical research and agronomy, but didn't disturb the basic division of labour between these areas. Music, agronomy and medical research are all fields with institutional structures to support innovation at the industry level (for example, music academies, municipal and central state patronage, music publishers, large orchestras with sufficient budget to commission new works, a trade press to cultivate and build up new movements, an instrument building industry oriented to integration with the consumers' tastes and with the composers' interests). But your argument is curiously divorced from the industry level. You don't really talk about rented housing or care for the elderly or crime prevention or health promotion or community development. These are the collective levels at which institutional support for innovation is needed and would have some effect, not the cross-industry field of foundations, which are simply a non-profit financial mechanism for supporting particular industries.

*Market structure*: You don't give much weight to competition at all. Most economists today reject Schumpeter's claim that a degree of monopoly is necessary, and while today many are readier to accept the case for collaborative networks at pre-competitive stage, during R&D and before bringing new products to market, most now think that over the product cycle and over the economic cycle, competition in the product market is the crucial spur, bringing together both opportunity and threat ("necessity is the mother of invention" and all that). The careful dovetailing of competition in supply and a modicum of mot-quite institutionalised collaboration in R&D – i.e. constantly patterns of who collaborates and how, but an accepted practice of doing somehow with at least some others – is now at the heart of all debate about government innovation policy and about innovation strategy in the business world. I still think there must be an equivalent in the welfare industries that foundations are interested in. Again, though, I doubt if you can say anything very intelligent about this without getting down to particular industries, such as crime prevention or employment services for people with mental health problems. Maybe at the very least you need some recommendations for more specific work on market structure and the relationship between the *different* forms of market structure that conduce to innovation at different stages in the product (service) cycle.

*Individual incentives*: Really innovative companies in the for-profit sector elicit innovation from staff by the use of incentives including part-share in proceeds from their innovations. Longer term incentives related to career interests are often crucial. What equivalent can foundations offer to "social entrepreneurs"? At present, they can only little more than status, which is a rather weak driver.

*Time horizons*: innovations differ hugely in the period over which they can prove themselves e.g. early intervention programmes (e.g. Perry School / High Scope, Surestart) may take twenty years show results. Only foundations can make those kinds of long term commitments to experiments, because governments never will. (I've even seen arguments of fundamental democratic principle, derived from Tom Paine's answer to Edmund Burke, to the effect that governments are the one sector in society that *should not* be that long termist, because it represents an unacceptable binding of and burdening of future generations that cannot be justified in the sector that relies upon coerced financing and coercive regulation.) This is in tension with the idea that may be read as implicit in some of the paper that innovation is a matter of a series of rapidly executed projects (e.g. your point about exit strategies being designed in early).

*Myths*: Most innovation is problem-based, but it is based on understandings of problems as open to agency, not just constrained by structure. Of course, seeing the world as agency-driven is the achievement of the weakly socially regulated solidarities, in Durkheimian terms; conversely, seeing it as dominated by structure is the work of the highly regulated solidarities. I think there is a need for a richer understanding of just how those solidarities are sustained at all in the welfare industries, because many of the institutions that govern those industries tend – for quite understandable social and political reasons – toward social regulation, which in turn squeezes innovative capacity. (There are of course innovations in social regulation in both the socially highly regulated solidarities, but anthropologists argue that they are on a quite separate cycle, because differently driven, from product and service innovation.)

*Consumer-driven innovation:* Many innovations are novel applications *by consumers* of novel techniques or products, unforeseen by the developers of the techniques or products (e.g. text messaging on mobile phones; the use of the internet for peer-to-peer networking of the kind that sustained Napster and its successors which is threatening the viability of the music industry). It's very hard to institutionalise that kind of innovation. What you can do – assuming that you want to encourage that kind of innovation at all, and I think there are good reasons for wanting it in many of the welfare industries that foundations are active in – is encourage people to develop new products that give more control and choice to their end-users. This puts a premium on innovations in choice-driven services.

*Evaluation:* The relationship with evaluation is crucial: innovation as a culture depends on the winnowing process, to which evaluation is critical. At present, the evaluation profession, in most of the industries in which non-profits are active, is geared to process evaluation, not product evaluation.

*Diffusion:* Is the diffusion stage of innovation none of the business of foundations? At times, you seem to imply that too much attention to it can take resources away from R&D. That might be the case for the individual foundation, but need not be the case for the foundation industry, if the industry is innovative in the development of collaborative organisations to support dissemination of evaluations of innovations and to support collaboration in projects at pre-competitive stage.

*"Learning by doing":* Arrow, and then more recently Solow, have argued that among the really important innovations in any field are the incremental ones of "learning by doing", which incrementally improve processes. Both the American and Japanese systems of manufacturing were built on precisely this. But much of the focus in the innovation literature has been on discontinuous innovations: economists in the Arrow-Solow school consider that if the arrival of those innovations is the

systematic effect of disciplines and institutions of creativity, this doesn't show up in the economic trend data, but that one can trace learning by doing innovations in ways that suggest that they are systematic and the result of institutions and disciplines.

*Labour intensive versus capital intensive innovation:* Most process innovations in the business world tend to be driven by the competitive economic pressures to raise productivity per factor of production (plant, worker, manager etc); in the fields that non-profits including foundations are active in, I wonder whether these pressures (a) operate as powerfully to create incentives and whether (b) they should do. For those who consider that the industries in which the welfare state and the non-profit sector have significant market share should be ones that create large numbers of jobs must also, logically, be extremely leery about productivity improvements that, at least in the short term, reduce the demand for labour by increasing the capital intensiveness of the technologies used, before such time as new product innovations have created new demand for new kinds of skills. These kinds of lags are ones that conventional market institutions cause, and one view of the foundation world is that part of its role might be to develop innovations that, at the very least, are not pro-cyclical in their effects on the demand for labour in the industries to which foundations are dedicated. One view of these industries is that they should be the labour market equivalent of the way environmentalists talk of forests as carbon "sinks" – partly protected zones of deliberately designed inefficiency (e.g. highly labour intensive production). If that view has anything going for it, then much of the innovation that is wanted in these fields will be counter-cyclical in labour market terms.

# References

Abramson, A. and Spann, J. (eds) (1998). *Foundations: Exploring their Unique Roles and Impacts in Society*. Washington, DC, Aspen Institute.

Alchon,G. (1985). *The Invisible Hand of Planning: Capitalism, Social Science and the State in the 1920's*. Princeton, NJ: Princeton University Press.

Aldrich, Howard (1999). *Organizations Evolving*. Thousand Oaks and London: Sage Publications.

Anheier, H. (ed.) (2000). *Third Way–Third Sector: Proceedings of a Policy Symposium Organised by the LSE Centre for Civil Society*. London: Centre for Civil Society, London School of Economics.

(2001). 'Foundations in Europe: A Comparative Perspective', in A. Schluter, V. Then, and P. Walkenhorst (eds), *Foundations in Europe, Society, Management and Law*. London, Directory of Social Change.

(2002). 'The Nonprofit Sector in Developed Market Economies: Between Government Reform and Civil Society'. Paper presented at seminar on Policy Platforms, Centre for Civil Society, London School of Economics (February).

and Kendall, J. (eds) (2001). *Third Sector Policy at the Crossroads: An International Nonprofit Analysis*. London: Routledge.

and List, R. (eds) (2000). Cross-Border Philanthropy. West Malling: Charities Aid Foundation.

and Toepler, S. (eds) (1999a). *Private Funds, Public Purpose*. New York: Kluwer Academic/Plenum Publishers.

Boulding, K. E. (1962). 'Notes on a Theory of Philanthropy', in F. G, Dickinson (ed.), *Philanthropy and Public Policy*. Washington, DC: National Bureau of Economic Research.

(1972). *Towards a Pure Theory of Foundations*. Danbury, CT: Nonprofit Report Inc.

(1973). *The Economy of Love and Fear: A Preface to Grants Economics*. Belmont, CA: Wadsworth.

Breiteneicher, C. K. and Marble, M. G. (2001). 'Strategic Programme Management', in A. Schluter, V. Then, and P. Walkenhorst (eds), *Foundations in Europe, Society, Management and Law*. London: Directory of Social Change.

Bremner, R. H. (1956). 'Scientific Philanthropy, 1873–1893', *Social Service Review*, 30: 168–73.

(1980). *The Public Good*. New York: Alfred A. Knopf.

Brown, G. (2000). *Goodman Lecture 2000*. London: National Council of Voluntary Organisations.

Brown, K., Kenny, S., Turner, B. with Prince, J. (2000). *Rhetorics of Welfare Uncertainty, Choice and Voluntary Associations*. Basingstoke: Macmillan.

Bruce, I. and Leat, D.(1993). *Management for Tomorrow*. London: VOLPROF, City University Business School.

Bulmer, M. (1999). 'Some Observations on the History of Large Philanthropic Foundations in Britain and The United States'. *Voluntas*, 6/3: 275–91.

Burkeman, S. (1999). *An Unsatisfactory Company? The 1999 Allen Lane Lecture*. London: The Allen Lane Foundation.

(1999b). 'Philanthropic Foundations: An International Perspective', in H. Anheier and S. Toepler (eds), *Private Funds, Public Purpose*. New York: Kluwer Academic/Plenum Publishers.

(1999c). 'Why Study Foundations?', in H. Anheier and S. Toepler (eds), *Private Funds, Public Purpose*. New York: Kluwer Academic/Plenum Publishers.

Arnove, R. (ed.) (1980). *Philanthropy and Cultural Imperialism: The Foundations at Home and Abroad*. Boston: GK Hall and Co.

Benington, J. (2000). 'Governing the Inter-relationships between State, Market and Civil Society', in H. Anheier (ed.), *Third Way–Third Sector: Proceedings of a Policy Symposium Organised by the LSE Centre for Civil Society*. London: Centre for Civil Society, London School of Economics.

Bertelsmann Foundation (ed.) (1999a). *The Future of Foundations in an Open Society*. Gütersloh: Bertelsmann Foundation Publishers.

(1999b). *Community Foundations in Civil Society*. Guetersloh, Bertelsmann.

Bolman, L. G. and Deal, T. E. (1991). *Reframing Organizations*. San Francisco: Jossey Bass.

Boris, E. T and Wolpert, J (2001). 'The Role of Philanthropic Foundations: Lessons from America's Experience With Private Foundations', in H. Anheier and J. Kendall (eds), *Third Sector Policy at the Crossroads: An International Nonprofit Analysis*. London: Routledge.

Bothwell, R. O. (2001). 'Trends in Self-Regulation and Transparency of Nonprofits in the US'. *The International Journal of Not-for-Profit Law*, 2/3.

Burlingame, D. (2001). 'Corporate Philanthropy's Future', in H. Anheier and J. Kendall (eds) (2001). *Third Sector Policy at the Crossroads: An International Nonprofit Analysis*. London: Routledge.

and Young, D. R. (1996). *Corporate Philanthropy at the Crossroads*. Bloomington and Indianapolis: Indiana University Press.

Cabinet Office (2002). *Private Action, Public Benefit. A Review of Charities and the Wider Not-for-profit Sector*. London. HM Government Strategy Unit Report, September.

Carlson, N. (2000). 'But Is It Smart Money? Nonprofits question the Value of Venture Philanthropy'. *Responsive Philanthropy*, Spring: 11–14.

Carrington, D. (2002) *The Investor Approach A Way Forward for the Community Fund?*, London: Community Fund.

Centre for Venture Philanthropy
www.pcf.org/pcfsite/stratphil/stratphillinks/definitions.html

Chesterman, M. (1979). *Charities, Trusts and Social Welfare*. London: Weidenfeld and Nicholson.

Clotfelter, C.T. and Ehrlich, T. (eds) (1999). *Philanthropy and the Nonprofit Sector in a Changing America*. Bloomington and Indianapolis: Indiana University Press.

Coleman, J. S., Menzel, H., and Katz, E. (1957). 'The Diffusion of an Innovation Among Physicians'. *Sociometry*, 20: 253–70.

Coser, Lewis (1965). 'Foundations as Gatekeepers of Contemporary Intellectual Life', in Lewis Coser (ed.), *Men of Ideas*. New York: Free Press.

Covington, S. (1994). *Community Foundations and Citizen Empowerment: Limited Support for Democratic Renewal*. Washington, DC: NCRP.

—— (1997). *Moving a Public Policy Agenda: The Strategic Philanthropy of Conservative Foundations*. Washington, DC: NCRP.

Curti, M.E. (1961). 'Tradition and Innovation in American Philanthropy'. *Proceedings of the American Philosophical Society*, 105/April: 145–56.

Dahrendorf, Lord R. (2001). *Goodman Lecture 2001*. London: National Council of Voluntary Organisations.

Deakin, N. (2001). *In Search of Civil Society*. London: Palgrave.

Directory of Social Change (2001/2002). *A Guide to Major Trusts* (3 vols). London: Directory of Social Change.

Dobkin-Hall, P. (1996). 'Research on the Charity World Should Offer Candor, Not a Whitewash'. *Chronicle of Philanthropy*, 11 January.

Douglas, J. and Wildavsky, A. (1980–1981). 'Big Government and the Private Foundations'. *Policy Studies Journal*, 9: 1175–90.

Dowie, M. (2001). *American Foundations: An Investigative History*. Cambridge, MA and London: MIT Press.

Elkington, J. (1998). *Cannibals With Forks: The Triple Bottom Line of 21st Century Business*. Gabriola Island, BC: New Society Publishers.

Emerson, J. and F. Twersky (1996). *New Social Entrepreneurs: The Success, Challenge and Lessons of Nonprofit Enterprise Creation*. San Francisco: The Roberts Foundations.

Ferlie, E. (ed.) (1996). *The New Public Management in Action*. Oxford: Oxford University Press.

Fischer, D. (1983). 'The Role of Philanthropic Foundations in the Reproduction and Production of Hegemony: Rockefeller Foundation and the Social Sciences'. *Sociology*, 17: 206–33.

Fitzherbert, L., Addison, D., and Rahman, E. (1999). *A Guide to the Major Trusts* (1990–2000 edn). London: Directory of Social Change.

and Eastwood, M. (eds) (1989). *A Guide to the Major Trusts* (1989 edn). London: Directory of Social Change.

Forrester, S, and Grau, J. (1997). *A Guide to the Major Trusts* (1997–8 edn). London: Directory of Social Change.

and Richards, G. (2001). A *Guide to the Major Trusts*, Vol. 1 (8th edn). London: Directory of Social Change.

Fleishman, J. L. (1999). 'Public Trust in Not-for-Profit Organisations and the Need for  Regulatory Reform', in C. T. Clotfelter and T. Ehrlich (eds), *Philanthropy and the Nonprofit Sector in a Changing America*. Bloomington and Indianapolis: Indiana University Press.

Flynn, P. and Hodgkinson, V. (eds) (2002). *Measuring the Impact of the Nonprofit Sector*. New York: Plenum/Kluwer.

Fowler, A. (1995). 'Assessing NGO Performance: Difficulties, Dilemmas and A Way Ahead', in M. Edwards and D. Hulme (eds), *Non-Governmental Organisations Performance and Accountability: Beyond the Magic Bullet*. London: Earthscan Publications.

Gaberman, B. (1999). Speech to 'Philanthropy Australia' conference, Sydney.

Gellner, E. (1994). *Conditions of Liberty: Civil Society and Its Rivals*. London: Hamish Hamilton.

Giddens, A. (1998). *The Third Way*. London: Polity Press.

(2001). 'The Role of the Third Sector in the Third Way', in H. Anheier (ed.), *Third Way–Third Sector: Proceedings of a Policy Symposium Organised by the LSE Centre for Civil Society*. London: Centre for Civil Society, London School of Economic.

Gronbjerg, K. A. (1998). 'Markets, Politics and Charity: Nonprofits in the Political Economy', in W. W. Powell and E. S. Clemens (eds), *Private Action and the Public Good*. New Haven: Yale University Press.

and Martell, L. with Paarlberg, L. (2000). 'Philanthropic Funding of Human Services: Solving Ambiguity Through the Two Stage Competitive Process'. *NonProfit and Voluntary Sector Quarterly*, 29/1: 9–40.

Henley Centre (1998). *Planning for Social Change 1998*. London: The Henley Centre.

Herberts, K. (2001). 'Finland', in A. Schluter, V. Then, and P. Walkenhorst (eds), *Foundations in Europe, Society, Management and Law*. London: Directory of Social Change.

Himmelstein, J. L. (1997). *Looking Good and Doing Good: Corporate Philanthropy and Corporate Power*. Bloomington and Indianapolis: Indiana University Press.

Hogwood, B. W. and Gunn, L. (1984). *Policy Analysis for the Real World*. Oxford: Oxford University Press.

Ilchman, W. F. and Burlingame, D. F. (1999). 'Accountability in a Changing Philanthropic Environment: Trustees and Self-Government at the End of the Century', in C. T. Clotfelter and T. Ehrlich (eds), *Philanthropy and the Nonprofit Sector in a Changing America*. Bloomington and Indianapolis: Indiana University Press.

Independent Sector (1994). *Giving and Volunteering 1994*. Washington, DC: Independent Sector.

International Network on Strategic Philanthropy. www.insp.efc.be/

Kanter, R. M. (1983). *The Change Masters*. New York: Simon and Schuster.

Stein, B.A., and Jick, T. D. (1992). *The Challenge of Organisational Change*. New York: The Free Press.

Karl, B. D. and Karl, A. W. (1999). 'Foundations and the Government: A Tale of Conflict and Consensus', in C. T. Clotfelter and T. Ehrlich (eds), *Philanthropy and the Nonprofit Sector in a Changing America*. Bloomington and Indianapolis: Indiana University Press.

and Katz, S. N. (1981). 'The American Private Philanthropic Foundations and the Public Sphere, 1980–1930'. *Minerva*, 19: 236–70.

Kendall, J. and Almond, S. (1998). *The UK Voluntary (Nonprofit) Sector in Comparative Perspective: Exceptional Growth and Transformation* (Working paper B051). London: Personal Social Services Research Unit, London School of Economics.

and Knapp, M. (1996). *The Voluntary Sector in the United Kingdom*. Manchester: Manchester University Press.

Koch-Weser, C. (1999). 'Foundations in the Developing World' in Bertelsmann Foundation (ed.), *The Future of Foundations in an Open Society*. Gütersloh: Bertelsmann Foundation Publishers.

Kramer, R. (1990). Change and 'Continuity in British Voluntary Organizations, 1976 to 1988'. *Voluntas*, 1/2: 33–60.

Lake, K., Reis, T, and Spann, J. (2000). 'From Grantmaking to Change Making: How the W. K. Kellogg Foundation's Impact Services Model Evolved to Enhance the Management and Social Effects of Large Initiatives'. *NonProfit and Voluntary Sector Quarterly*, 29/1: 41–68.

Landry, C. (2000). *The Creative City: A Toolkit for Urban Innovators*. London: Comedia, Earthscan Publications Ltd.

Leat, D. (1992). *Trusts in Transition: The Policy and Practice of Grant-Giving Trusts*. York: Joseph Rowntree Foundation.

(1996). 'British Foundations: The Organisation and Management of Grantmaking'. *Voluntas*, 6/3: 317–29.

(1998). *Faith, Hope and Information: Assessing a Grant Application*. York: Joseph Rowntree Foundation.

(1999). 'British Foundations. The Organisation and Management of Grant-Making', in H. Anheier and S. Toepler (eds), *Private Funds, Public Purpose*. New York: Kluwer /Plenum.

(2001). 'United Kingdom', in A. Schluter, V. Then, and P. Walkenhorst (eds), *Foundations in Europe, Society, Management and Law*. London: Directory of Social Change.

Letts, C., Ryan, W. and Grossman, A. (1997). 'Virtuous Capital: What Foundations can Learn from Venture Capitalists'. *Harvard Business Review*, March/April: 36–44.

Lewis, J. (1999). 'Reviewing the Relationship Between Voluntary Sector and the State in Britain in the 1990s'. *Voluntas*, 10/3: 255–70.

Logan, D. (2002). *Corporate Citizenship: Defining Terms and Scoping Key Issues*. London: Corporate Citizenship Company.

MacDonald, Dwight (1956). *The Ford Foundation: The Men and the Millions*. New York: Reynal and Co.

McIlnay, D. P. (1998). *How Foundations Work*. San Francisco: Jossey Bass.

McLean, I. and Johnes, M. (2000). *Aberfan Government and Disasters*. Cardiff: Welsh Academic Press.

McMenamin, B. (1997). 'Trojan Horse Money'. *Forbes*, 16 December.

Middleton, M. (1987). 'Nonprofit Boards of Directors: Beyond the Governance Function, in W. W. Powell (ed.), *The Nonprofit Sector: A Research Handbook*. New Haven: Yale University Press.

Mohn, R. (1999). 'Welcome Address' in Bertelsmann Foundation (ed.), *The Future of Foundations in an Open Society*. Gütersloh: Bertelsmann Foundation Publishers.

Mulgan, G. (2000). 'Government and the Third Sector: Building A More Equal Partnership', in H. Anheier (ed.), *Third Way–Third Sector: Proceedings of a Policy Symposium Organised by the LSE Centre for Civil Society*. London: Centre for Civil Society, London School of Economics.

Nagai, A., Lerner, R., and Rothman, S. (1994). *Giving for Social Change: Foundations, Public Policy and the American Political Agenda*. Westport, CT: Praeger Publishers.

Nason, J. (1977). *Trustees and the Future of Foundations*. New York: Council on Foundations.

(1989). *Foundation Trusteeship: Service in the Public Interest*. New York: Foundation Center.

NCRP (National Committee for Responsive Philanthropy) (1991). *California Community Foundation and the Disadvantaged: No Focus, Marginal Impact*. Washington, DC: NCRP.

(1994). *Ten Top Community Foundations Responsiveness to Low Income and other Historically Disenfranchised Groups in American Society*. Washington, DC: NCRP.

(1997). *Moving a Public Policy Agenda: The Strategic Philanthropy of Conservative Foundations*. Washington, DC: NCRP.

(2000). 'Alternative Funds or Community Foundations: Which Are a Better Philanthropic Investment?', *NCRP Quarterly*.

Nielsen, W. (1972). *The Big Foundations*. New York: Columbia University Press.

(1979). *The Endangered Sector*. New York: Columbia University Press.

(1985). *The Golden Donors*. New York: Truman Talley Books/EP Dutton.

(1996). *Inside American Philanthropy: The Dramas of Donorship*. Norman: University of Oklahoma Press.

Odendahl, T. (ed.) (1987a). *America's Wealthy and the Future of Foundations*. New York: The Foundation Center.

(1987b). 'Wealthy Donors and their Charitable Attitudes', in T. Odendahl (ed.), *America's Wealthy and the Future of Foundations*. New York: The Foundation Center.

(1990). *Charity Begins at Home: Generosity and Self Interest Among the Philanthropic Elite*. New York: Basic Books.

and Boris, E. T. (1983). 'A Delicate Balance: Foundation Board-Staff Relations'. *Foundation News*, 24/3 (Council on Foundations, Washington DC).

and Daniels, A. (1985). *Working in Foundations*. New York: Foundation Center.

Olasky (1992). The Tragedy of American Passion. Washington D.C., Regnery Gateway.

Osborne, S. (1998). *Voluntary Organisations and Innovation in Public Services*. London: Routledge.

Ostrander, S.A. (1993). 'Diversity and Democracy in Philanthropic Organisations: The Case of the Haymarket People's Fund', in D. R. Young *et al.* (eds), *Governing, Leading and Managing Nonprofit Organizations*. San Francisco: Jossey Bass.

(1994). 'Charitable Foundations, Social Movements and Social Justice Funding', in J. H. Stansfield II (ed.), *The Non-profit Sector and Social Justice*. Indianapolis: Indiana University Press.

and Schervish, P.G. (1990). 'Giving and Getting: Philanthropy as a Social Relation', in J. Van Til et al. (eds), *Critical Issues in American Philanthropy: Strengthening Theory and Practice*. San Francisco: Jossey Bass.

Ostrower, F. (1987). 'The Role of Advisors to the Wealthy', in T. Odendahl (ed.), *America's Wealthy and the Future of Foundations*. New York: The Foundation Center.

(1995). *Why the Wealthy Give: The Culture of Elite Philanthropy*. Princeton, NJ: Princeton University Press.

Perrow, C. (2001). 'The Rise of Nonprofits and the Decline of Civil Society', in H. Anheier (ed.), *Organisational Theory and the Non-profit*

*Form*. London: Centre for Civil Society Report 2, London School of Economics.

Peterson Commission (1970). *Foundations, Private Giving and Public Policy: Recommendations of the Commission on Foundations and Private Philanthropy*. Chicago and London: University of Chicago Press.

Pharoah, C. and Siederer, N. (1997). 'Numbers, Income, Assets: New Numbers', in C. Pharoah and M. Smerdon (eds), *Dimensions of the Voluntary Sector*. West Malling: Charities Aid Foundation.

Pifer, A. (1984a). *Speaking Out: Reflections on Thirty Years of Foundation Work*. Washington, DC: Council on Foundations.

Pifer, A. (1984b) 'Twenty Years in Retrospect: A Personal View', in A. Pifer (ed.), *Philanthropy in an Age of Transition*. New York Foundation Center.

Pifer, A. (1984c). 'Foundations and Public Policy Formulation', in A. Pifer (ed.), *Philanthropy in an Age of Transition*. New York: Foundation Center.

Pinter, F. (2001). 'Funding Global Civil Society Organisations', in H. Anheier, M. Glasius, and M. Kaldor (eds), *Global Civil Society 2001*. Oxford: Oxford University Press.

Plowden, W. (2001). *Next Steps in Voluntary Action*. London: London Centre for Civil Society and NCVO.

Porter, M. E. and Kramer, M.R. (1999). 'Philanthropy's New Agenda: Creating Value'. *Harvard Business Review*, November/December: 121–30.

Powell, W.W. (ed.) (1987). *The Nonprofit Sector: A Research Handbook*. New Haven and London: Yale University Press.

and DiMaggio, P. (1991). *The New Institutionalism in Organisational Analysis*. Chicago: University of Chicago Press.

Prewitt, K. (1999). 'The Importance of Foundations in an Open Society', in Bertelsmann Foundation (ed.), *The Future of Foundations in an Open Society*. Gütersloh: Bertelsmann Foundation Publishers.

Prochaska, F. K. (1990). 'Philanthropy', in F. M. L. Thompson (ed.), *The Cambridge Social History of Britain 1750–1950, Vol. 3*. Cambridge: Cambridge University Press.

Reeves, T. C. (1969). *Freedom and the Foundation: The Fund for the Republic in the Era of McCarthyism*. New York: Albert K. Knopf.

Reis, T and Clohsey, S. J. (2001). 'Unleashing New Resources and Entrepreneurship for the Common Good: A Philanthropic Renaissance', in A. Schluter, V. Then, and P. Walkenhorst (eds), *Foundations in Europe, Society, Management and Law*, London, Directory of Social Change.

Renz, L. (1997). *International Grant Making: A Report on US Foundations*. New York: Foundation Centre.

(2002). *Foundation Giving*. New York: Foundation Centre.

*et al.* (1997). *Foundation Giving: Yearbook of Facts and Figures on Private, Corporate and Community Foundations*. New York: Foundation Center.

Ridings, D. (1999). 'The Legitimization of Foundation Work' in Bertelsmann Foundation (ed.), *The Future of Foundations in an Open Society*. Gütersloh: Bertelsmann Foundation Publishers.

Rimel, R.W. (1999). Strategic Philanthropy: Pew's Approach to Matching Needs with Resources. Philiadelphia: Pew Charitable Trust.

Roelefs, J. (1984/5). 'Foundations and the Supreme Court'. *Telos*, 62: 59–87.

Romanelli, Elaine (1991). 'The Evolution of Organisational Forms'. *Annual Review of Sociology*, 17: 79–103.

Rose-Ackerman, S. (1996). 'Altruism, Nonprofits and Economic Theory'. *Journal of Economic Literature*, 34: 701–28.

Salamon, L. (1987). 'Partners in Public Service', in W.W. Powell (ed.), *The Nonprofit Sector: A Research Handbook*. New Haven: Yale University Press.

Salamon, L. (1992) "Foundations as investment managers: part I. The process" *Nonprofit Management and Leadership* 3(2), 117-137.

Salamon, L. M. (1997). *Holding the Center: America's Nonprofit Sector at a Crossroads*. New York: The Nathan Cummings Foundation.

and Anheier, H. (1994). 'In Search of the Non-profit Sector. I: The Question of Definitions'. *Voluntas*, 3/2: 125–52.

(1996). *Social Origins of Civil Society: Exploring the Nonprofit Sector Cross Nationally* (Working papers of the Johns Hopkins Nonprofit Sector Project). Baltimore, MD: Institute for Policy Studies, Johns Hopkins University.

(1997). *Defining the Nonprofit Sector*. Manchester: Manchester University Press.

Schuman, M. (1998). 'Why Do Progressive Foundations Give Too Little to Too Many?' *The Nation*, 12 January.

Siederer, N. (1996). 'Giving in Trust, The Role of the Grantmaking Trust', in C. Hanvey and T. Philpot (eds), *Sweet Charity*. London: Routledge.

Sievers, B. (1997). 'If Pigs had Wings'. *Foundations News and Commentary*, November/December.

Simon, J.G. (1996). 'The Regulation of American Foundations: Looking Backward at the Tax Reform Act of 1969'. *Voluntas*, 6/3: 243–54.

Smith, J. A. and Borgmann, K. (2001). 'Foundations in Europe: The Historical Context', in A. Schluter, V. Then, and P. Walkenhorst (eds), *Foundations in Europe, Society, Management and Law*. London: Directory of Social Change.

Smyth, J. (2000). *The Guide to UK Company Giving*. London: Directory of Social Change.

Stanfield , S. (ed) (1995). Nonprofit Organizations and Social Justice, San Francisco: Jossey-Bass Publishers.

Tracey Garey Changemakers. http://www.changemakers.net/

Troyer, T. (2000). *The 1969 Private Foundation Law: Historical Perspectives on Its Origins and Underpinnings*. Washington, DC: Council on Foundations.

UNDP (United Nations Development Programme) (2002). *The Human Development Report*. New York: United Nations.

Unwin, J. and Westland, P. (1997). *Local Funding: The Impact of the National Lottery Charities Board*. London: Association of Charitable Foundations.

Van Til, J. and Associates (eds) (1990). *Critical Issues in American Philanthropy*. San Francisco: Jossey Bass.

Villemur, A. (ed.) (1995). *A Directory of Grant-making Trusts*. West Malling, Charities Aid Foundation.

Vincent, J. and Pharoah, C. (2000). *Patterns of Independent Grant-Making in the UK, Dimensions 2000, Vol. 3*. West Malling: Charities Aid Foundation.

Weick, K (1995). *Sensemaking in Organizations*. California: Sage Publications Inc.

Whitaker, B. (1979). *The Foundations: An Anatomy of Philanthropic Societies*. New York: Pelican Books.

Whitaker, B. (1974) *The Philanthropoids*, New York, William Morrow.

Williams, R. (1998). 'Know Thy Critics'. *Foundation News and Commentary*, May/June, 25–9.

Wolpert, J. (1995) 'Delusions of Charity,' *American Prospect*, pp. 86-88.

Yeo, S. (2002). *Mutualism and Cooperatives in Britain* (Report No. 4). London: Centre for Civil Society, London School of Economics.

Ylvisaker, P. (1987). 'Foundations and Nonprofit Organisations', in W.W. Powell (ed.), The Nonprofit Sector: A Research Handbook. New Haven and London: Yale University Press.

# About the authors

Helmut K. Anheier (Ph.D. Yale) is Centennial Professor at the London School of Economics and, and full professor at UCLA's School of Public Policy and Social Research. Prior to this he was Director of LSE's Centre for Civil Society (1998-2002), Reader of Social Policy at LSE (1998-2001), Senior Research Associate at the Johns Hopkins University Institute for Policy Studies, Associate Professor of Sociology at Rutgers University, and Social Affairs Officer at the United Nations. He has also held research appointments at Yale University, the University of Cologne, and the Science Center in Berlin. Dr. Anheier's work has focused on civil society, the nonprofit sector, philanthropy, organizational studies, policy analysis and comparative methodology. He is a founding editor of *Voluntas*, and author of over 200 publications in several languages.

Diana Leat is currently Visiting Research Fellow at the Centre for Civil Society at the London School of Economics. In addition to academic appointments, Diana has been a consultant to various grantmaking foundations in the UK and Australia reviewing their policies and practices. For the last 3 years Diana has spent various periods in Australia, most recently as Senior Research Fellow at Deakin University with Philanthropy Australia working on a study of foundation stakeholders, governance and accountability. She has also worked on a world-wide collection of case studies of community foundation support organizations for WINGS-CF. Diana has published extensively on the voluntary sector, foundations and social policy.

# Recent Comedia titles

**Reflections on urban lighting: An aesthetic and socio-cultural approach**

**By Zenobia Razis**

'Reflections on urban lighting' discusses an under-explored problem and opportunity. It assesses how in places as diverse as Japan, Europe and the US urban public space has been transformed since cities were lit by electricity for the first time in the 19<sup>th</sup> century. It looks at the connection between technical possibilities and the aesthetics employed through artificial lighting. It argues that natural light originally and artificial lighting subsequently is linked symbolically, philosophically and aesthetically with the entire course and ideals of Western civilisation. Four ways of how the city is perceived are discussed: 'the city as décor', 'as museum', 'as a canvas' and 'as democratic space'.

The dynamics of the day-time city and the city of the night are contrasted and how the idea of 'bright lights' is seen as a measure of a city's development especially advertising illumination with Las Vegas the example par excellence. Lighting has become central to urban image making with its link to the concept of the 24 hour city and the tourism industry. Yet there are environmental and cultural consequences of over-illumination and light pollution but no adequate legal framework to guide the expansion of lighting.

Urban lighting is rarely addressed in an integrated way apart from in relation to lighting and safety. A piecemeal approach is adopted whereby specific needs are addressed, such as road lighting, without considering its overall visual effect or impacts on pedestrians and the cityscape. The book argues that there should be a more ecological approach to lighting more in harmony with nature as well as a new philosophy that uses light to create democratic public space.

**ISBN 1 837667 11 6    120 pages          £9.00**


## Culture at the Crossroads: Culture and cultural institutions at the beginning of the 21<sup>st</sup> century

**By Marc Pachter and Charles Landry**

'Culture at the Crossroads' re-imagines the 21$^{st}$ century cultural landscape and seeks to be a guide through its complexities. It explores the disquiet on the cultural front setting out the new terms for debating the role of culture and cultural institutions in an era where the market seems to dominate our thinking. It highlights the strategic issues that culture needs to face such as: how is cultural insight projected; how institutions can communicate iconically; whether cultural leadership and authority are valid ideas in the contemporary world; how qualities of quality can be understood; what the real difference is between the 'real' or virtual and fake; what an inclusive culture could represent and how the relation between artists and society can be rethought.

*"The discussions on which 'Culture at the Crossroads' is based were one of the most stimulating occasions I have experienced, provoking deep thought about how culture has changed in the last half century and how cultural institutions have — and should — be responding to such changes."*

**Charles Saumarez Smith**, director of the National Gallery, London

**ISBN 1 873667 13 2  114pages      £9.00**

**Making Sense of Place: New Approaches to Place Marketing**
**By Chris Murray**

This innovative book shows what the new place marketing could be. It reveals a strong and persistent tendency in UK place marketing literature to:

- focus on the past and be generally backward-looking;
- represent places as culturally homogeneous; and
- not to show diversity or distinctiveness, but to promote a similar, bland mix of facilities and attractions for every area.

It highlights that there is an important and potentially volatile difference between marketing products and services and marketing something as complex as a 'place'. The identities of British cities and regions being peddled are at best partial and at worst completely fictitious. The pages of brochures are crowded with images of the past – 85% of the sample has a heritage theme for the cover, people in historic costume, knights in armour, gentle country peasants and local fisher-folk enjoying a pipe at dusk with their dog on the quayside. This would not be a problem if the images were balanced with others, but generally they are not.

Making Sense of Place explores the landscape of place marketing suggesting what it could become and how it can be rethought and reinvigorated

**ISBN 1 873667 18 3  120 pages     £9.00**

**The Creative City: A toolkit for urban innovators**
**By Charles Landry**

Drawing on examples from around the world 'The Creative City' sets out a new radical vision for cities and how decision makers and citizens can think, plan and act creatively in finding imaginative solutions to their problems. *'The Creative City will be one of the key urban texts of the next decade. It is a truly millennial book and shows how new modes of thinking can help regenerate cities facing the challenge of survival.'*- Sir Peter Hall, Bartlett Professor of Planning, University College, London. **ISBN 1 85383 613 3  300 pages    £19.95**